Aimee Ray's
SWEET & SIMPLE JEWELRY

Aimee Ray's
SWEET & SIMPLE JEWELRY

· 17 Designers, 10 Techniques & 32 Projects to Make ·

Aimee Ray with Kathy Sheldon

LARK JEWELRY
& BEADING

LARK JEWELRY & BEADING

An Imprint of Sterling Publishing
387 Park Avenue South
New York, NY 10016

ISBN 978-1-4547-0792-9

Distributed in Canada by Sterling Publishing
c/o Canadian Manda Group, 165 Dufferin Street
Toronto, Ontario, Canada M6K 3H6
Distributed in the United Kingdom by GMC Distribution Services
Castle Place, 166 High Street, Lewes, East Sussex, England BN7 1XU
Distributed in Australia by Capricorn Link (Australia) Pty. Ltd.
P.O. Box 704, Windsor, NSW 2756, Australia

For information about custom editions, special sales, and premium and corporate purchases, please contact Sterling Special Sales at 800-805-5489 or specialsales@sterlingpublishing.com.

Email academic@larkbooks.com for information about desk and examination copies. The complete policy can be found at larkcrafts.com.

Every effort has been made to ensure that all the information in this book is accurate. However, due to differing conditions, tools, and individual skills, the publisher cannot be responsible for any injuries, losses, and other damages that may result from the use of the information in this book.

Manufactured in China

2 4 6 8 10 9 7 5 3 1

larkcrafts.com

30

32

35

39

42

44

47

50

53

56

58

60

63

64

66

69

72

75

78

81

84

88

92

94

96

98

101

106

110

114

Contents

118

120

Introduction

Welcome to *Aimee Ray's Sweet & Simple Jewelry*! I'm so excited to bring it to you. My ventures into jewelry making began when I was a kid and learned to finger crochet. I made one loooong chain and looped it around and around my neck. After that, I progressed to braiding friendship bracelets and logged many hours on those until friendship grew to love when I discovered beaded necklaces and bracelets. I still can't pass the bead aisle of a craft store without hearing them call out to me!

The idea for this book came about the day my editor, Kathy Sheldon, and I both confessed that one of our favorite procrastination techniques is scrolling through the many fresh and fun jewelry designs for sale online. The sheer variety of materials and techniques used in these pieces is so inspiring. We realized a book of projects based on some of our favorite pieces would offer crafters a great way to get started with jewelry-making while giving experienced jewelers a chance to work with materials and techniques they may not have tried before.

So jump in and enjoy. If you're a pro at embroidery, but you've never made jewelry before, the Basics section starting on page 10 will teach you what you need to know. If you've made plenty of jewelry but you've never embroidered, needle-felted, made molds to cast cabochons, baked shrink plastic, or worked with polymer clay, we've got you covered, too.

Or skip the Basics altogether, flip through to find your favorite project, and start making! Each project tells you everything you need in terms of tools and materials (feel free to substitute to suit your own style), and has step-by-step instructions. If templates, patterns, or graphics are needed, you'll find them at the back of the book.

Big thanks to the generous and talented designers for sharing their creative processes with us. You'll find out more about them starting on page 126. Visit their blogs and online shops to see more of their work. And enjoy making and wearing your own sweet & simple jewelry!

Basics

This book casts a wide net over all kinds of jewelry that's popular right now. Many different techniques and materials are used, but you don't need to be a master jeweler to make any project in this book. It's really just a matter of materials + tools + techniques = awesome piece of jewelry, and that's exactly what's covered in this chapter.

Materials

You probably already have or are familiar with many of the materials used to make the projects in the book. Skim through the projects, decide where you want to start, and then check out this section to learn more about specific materials.

Felt

Felt is a wonderful material to use in jewelry making because it's soft and flexible and doesn't fray. It's hard to beat the look of 100 percent wool felt (see the Lazy Daisy Cuff, page 110), but you can use polyester felt (which is easier to find in stores) instead.

Fabric

Some of the projects in this book call for fabric. The Fabric Scrap Necklaces (page 58), true to their name, require only whatever scraps you have on hand. The cross-stitched pieces on pages 81 and 88 use embroidery fabric (available in fabric shops and craft stores). This fabric has the same number of horizontal and vertical threads per inch, which helps you keep your stitches all the same size. Such fabric is categorized by count (which equals the threads per inch), ranging from 11 to 40 count.

Fabric Pens and Disappearing Fabric Markers

These tools are handy for tracing template shapes or embroidery patterns onto fabric.

Embroidery Floss

Embroidery floss comes in small bundles, or skeins. A strand of floss is made up of six threads twisted together. For a thick embroidered line, use all six. For more delicate work, separate the threads and use two or three. The trick to separating the

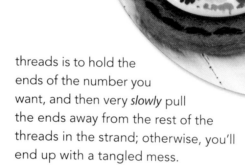

threads is to hold the ends of the number you want, and then very *slowly* pull the ends away from the rest of the threads in the strand; otherwise, you'll end up with a tangled mess.

Embroidery Hoop

Plastic or wooden embroidery hoops have two round frames that fit together and tighten with a screw. Hooping your fabric will give you a tight, smooth surface to stitch on, and will prevent puckering. Plastic hoops are a good investment because they're sturdier than wood ones and will last a long time. You can use different-size hoops for different-size projects, but a 6-inch (15.2 cm) one works well for almost anything.

Beads

Ah, beads. Made from glass, crystal, pearl, wood, metal, or plastic, beads have such an effect on the mood of a piece of jewelry. Let the beads used in these projects inspire you, but don't fret if you can't find the exact same ones. Instead, customize to match your personality and wardrobe. Beads are usually measured in millimeters, not inches. The millimeter measurement generally refers to the diameter of the bead. Seed beads are sized by number: the higher the number, the smaller the bead.

Cabochons and Cameos

Cabochon refers to a nondrilled bead that's flat on one side and typically domed on the other. Jewelry making with cabochons is easy because you usually just glue them into bezels or settings. You can find wonderful vintage and reproduction flower-shaped cabochons online, and many bead shops carry them, too. We've even found inexpensive packages of plastic flower cabochons in the scrapbooking section of craft stores (see Super Simple Flower Posts, page 63). Cameos and domed cabochons with decals are also popular and easy to find online. Check out page 24 for instructions on how to use vintage cabochons to make your own molds and then create your own flower or cameo cabochons. It's really fun and a lot easier than you'd think!

Buttons

Buttons are a fun alternative to beads and are available in all sorts of colors, sizes, shapes, and patterns.

Inexpensive kits available in fabric stores make it super easy to make your own fabric-covered buttons. Don't forget that in addition to taking the place of a bead, a button can also serve as a clasp (see Wrapped Bead Bracelet, page 35).

Charms, Pendants, and Stones

Purchased charms and pendants (such as the leaf in the Felted Acorn Necklace, page 53, or the Foxy Pendant on page 106) can be used to embellish your projects or can even be the focal point. Vintage glass stones in settings with loops make for quick design elements. You can find all of these online as well as in bead shops and craft stores.

Filigree Shapes

Filigree shapes are handy in jewelry making because you can adhere them to blanks or link them together with jump rings. You can add beads to them easily or glue cabochons onto them. Find them in bead shops or online.

Wool Roving

Used in needle felting, roving is carded wool drawn into long continuous strands. As needle felting has gained in popularity, roving is easier to find—

look for it online or in craft stores and yarn shops. See Needle Felting (page 26) for information on this technique.

Two-Part Silicone Molding Putty

This stuff is amazing! It comes in two parts, and you simply knead the parts together for a putty that makes it simple to create molds so you can cast your own flowers, cameos, and more. See page 24 for more information.

Polymer Clay

Even if you've never used polymer clay before, pick some up the next time you're in a craft shop—it's a wonderfully versatile material to use in jewelry making. Polymer clay contains polyvinyl chloride (PVC), a plasticizer to make it pliable at room temperature, and color pigments. Once baked, it becomes permanently hard. Polymer clay needs to be conditioned before you use it: for the small amounts needed to make the projects in this book, you can simply roll a small amount into a ball, then rub it between your palms into a long snake. Fold it back on itself, roll it out again, and continue until the clay is soft and even in color and consistency.

Air-Dry Clay

Air-dry clay is a material that can be sculpted, shaped, molded, or used to fill a bezel and will adhere to most surfaces without the use of an adhesive. It air-dries (without baking) to a hard finish similar to that of soft wood and can be carved or sanded and decorated with any kind of paint.

Epoxy Clay

Epoxy clay is a self-hardening material that comes in two parts: a resin (often with color added) and a hardener. To use the clay you simply knead equal amounts of the two parts together. Then you can mold it into a flower or cameo, shape it into a bead, or use it to fill a bezel. There's no need for firing or baking—it cures to a hard, permanent state in about 24 hours.

Shrink Plastic

You'll be surprised by all the ways you can use shrink plastic to make jewelry. Available in craft stores, art supply stores, and online, shrink plastic comes in thin sheets that bake down to about a third their original size but nine times as thick. Using shrink plastic is as easy as sanding it (unnecessary if you purchase the pre-roughened kind); drawing, tracing, or photocopying a design onto it; cutting your design out; baking it; and sealing it.

Miscellaneous Doodads

If you look beyond the typical jewelry supplies, you'll discover all kinds of things that can be used to make jewelry. Items such as the dome in the Terrarium Necklace (page 44) and the little corked bottle for the Dandelion Wish Necklace (page 118) can be found online and in larger craft stores. Experiment!

Findings

Findings, the small, typically metal components used to assemble jewelry, are the worker bees of this craft—without them, your pieces would quite literally fall apart. It's easy to find a huge selection of findings made from all kinds of metal (and at all price ranges) in beads stores, craft stores, and online.

Jump rings are circular wire loops used to make simple connections in jewelry. Learn the correct way to open and close a jump ring (see page 28), and you'll have mastered one key to making jewelry.

Clasps are typically used to open or close the chain, wire, or cord on a piece of jewelry. The range of clasp designs available is inspiring: lobster, toggle, S-hook, box, magnetic, and even plain snaps. Purchasing a special clasp is an easy way to give a necklace or bracelet a little extra pizzazz.

Head pins are lengths of thin wires with either a flat or a ball head on one end to keep beads or other objects from sliding off. You can wrap or loop the end of the wire to make a component for your jewelry (see page 28). **Eye pins** come with a small loop at one end that serves as a built-in connection.

Bead caps are typically metal and usually are strung above or below a round bead. Often an afterthought, decorative bead caps (such as the ones used in the Lolita Earrings, above) can play an important role in the look of your finished piece.

Pin backs, used to make brooches and pins, come in several shapes and sizes. They can be sewn to fabric pieces or glued to metal ones.

Earring findings come in various shapes, including French wires, kidney wires, lever backs, hoops, and posts (also called studs). Experiment to discover which kinds of earring findings look best with both your earring design and your earlobes!

Bezels are metal cups into which stones or cabochons are set. A bezel may serve as a pendant, be built onto a ring, or come with loops attached so it can be used as a link in a bracelet, necklace, or earrings.

Settings are metal components similar to bezels in that they form a frame (often round or oval) for a cabochon. Be sure to size your setting—usually measured in millimeters—to your cabochon. Many of the settings used in the projects in this book are lace-edged settings—the loops of the "lace" make for easy jewelry assembly. With cup lace-edge settings, the lace edges are perpendicular to the setting's flat surface and form a kind of bezel for a cabochon. Even if the fit is snug, use adhesive to secure the cabochon to the setting.

Ring blanks are available in many different finishes and are usually adjustable. Some have a flat top that you can glue items to, and some have a bezel top so you can embed items.

Hair pin findings can be found at craft stores and online. They typically have a round (sometimes filigreed) surface that you can glue a cabochon onto.

Stringing Materials

Your choice of material for stringing your pieces can greatly influence the feel of the final piece: Explore all the different types of chain and wire at your bead or craft shop, and consider a natural cord for a rustic feel or ribbon for a softer look.

Chain is made up of connected (usually metal) links, which may be round, oval, twisted, or hammered. Ball chain (what you pull to turn on a lamp) is a simple, inexpensive chain that's popular now.

Wire comes in different diameters, known as *gauge*. The smaller the gauge number, the heavier the wire.

Ribbon is another attractive (and easy!) alternative to chain or wire. It looks especially nice with fabric pieces (see the Fabric Scrap Pendants, page 58).

Hemp, bamboo, or leather cord is an alternative to chain or wire that can give a nice natural look to your jewelry. You can find cord at bead shops and in craft stores in natural or fun, bright colors.

Adhesives

Fabric glue, white school glue, cyanoacrylate glue, and **jewelry adhesive** are all called for in various projects in this book. If a particular type of adhesive is needed, the project will specify that in its materials list. See Gluing Jewelry Components (at right) for tips on using adhesives.

Resin

Resin provides a clear, hard, protective finish, and is great for making pendants with graphics, such as the Foxy Pendant (below). You can find many different types and brands of resin. The instructions on page 107 are a great starting point, and you can even experiment with substituting colored resin for clay when casting cabochons (page 24).

Paints and Sealants

Use paints to embellish your projects (such as the Painted Picture Choker, page 120) and sealants to protect them. The specific type of paint or sealant you should use can be found in the projects' materials lists.

GLUING JEWELRY COMPONENTS

It's worth taking extra care when adhering pieces so your jewelry will last a long time. Always follow the manufacturer's directions for the particular adhesive you're using. But in general, follow these guidelines:

• Make sure your adhesive is compatible with any material it will come into contact with: Some types of glues will react with the finish of beads or other components.

• First clean all surfaces to be joined with rubbing alcohol applied to a cotton swab. You may also want to roughen the surfaces of metal or other parts with fine sandpaper.

• Apply the adhesive to the smaller of two surfaces to be joined.

• Spread a thin layer of adhesive on the entire surface, getting as close to any edges as possible.

• Wipe any excess glue off immediately using the end of a toothpick.

• Allow for adequate drying time; even longer than the directions state is usually best.

Tools

You won't need a bunch of expensive or exotic tools to make these projects. In fact, you probably already own most of what you need.

Pliers and Cutters

Chain-nose pliers may be the most versatile tool for making jewelry. Their jaws taper to a point on the outside with a flat surface on the inside, which makes them great for opening jump rings (use two, one for each end of the jump ring) and making bends in wire 1 .

Round-nose pliers have round, tapered jaws that are perfect for making wire loops. Where you place the wire on the tapered jaws will determine the size of your loops 2 .

Flat-nose pliers, which have flat, non-tapered jaws, are helpful for bending wire and holding it steady as you make wire wraps or loops 3 .

Wire cutters have very sharp blades that come to a point. Use wire cutters to trim craft wire, head pins, and eye pins 4 .

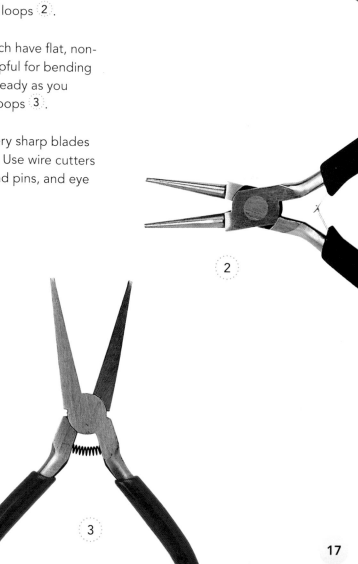

Embroidery Needles

Choose an embroidery needle with a sharp point and a hole, or eye, that's large enough to thread with floss easily. You'll want a needle with a larger eye if you're using all six plies of floss and one with a smaller eye if you're using three plies or fewer. It's a good idea to buy packs of several different sizes of embroidery needles so you have a variety to choose from.

Scissors and Pinking Shears

Along with craft scissors, make sure you have a good pair of fabric scissors for cutting felt and fabric. While you may be able to get away with cutting fabric using your household scissors, don't ever use your fabric shears to cut paper—the fiber in the paper will quickly dull their blades! Small curved scissors (embroidery scissors or even manicure scissors) are handy for cutting intricate shapes, and pinking shears create a zigzag edge, which both keeps fabric from fraying and looks cute.

Hole Punches

Hole punches cut perfect little circles easily. Sturdier punches are great because you can use them on felt or shrink plastic as well as paper.

Smoothing Tools

Files, sandpaper, and emery boards can be used to smooth rough edges and sharp points.

Needle-Felting Needle and Foam

The basic needle-felting needle is 3½ to 4 inches (8.9 to 10.2 cm) long and made of steel. It has a very sharp point and little barbs along the edges. These barbs latch onto the felt or wool roving and tangle and enmesh the layers to create a firm, three-dimensional shape. Be careful when felting—these needles are extremely sharp!

If you're covering a large area, a multi-needle tool (including the newer, pen-like one) is handy. These tools typically hold three or four needles and are easy to hold and use. The wooden-handled version can hold even more needles for even faster felting. You can switch needles in and out with these multi-needle tools, in case one breaks or you need to change needle sizes.

You can buy special foam made for needle felting, but dense, 2-inch (5.1 cm) thick upholstery foam works just as well. Use this to support your felt as you work and to keep the felting needle from piercing your table-top (or hands!). See page 26 for more on needle-felting techniques.

Techniques

Embroidery Essentials

If you're an old hand at embroidery, you can probably skip this section. If you've never tried it, these jewelry projects are a great place to start!

Transferring Templates and Patterns

For the projects in this book, try one of the two methods below to transfer the embroidery patterns to the fabric or felt:

• Light Method: Tracing patterns using a light table or a sunny window works well for most light-colored, lightweight fabrics. Tape your pattern to the light table or window and secure the fabric on top so you can see the lines through it. Use any pencil or fabric pen (including a disappearing one) to trace the lines.

• Tissue Paper Method: You can trace your pattern onto thin paper such as tissue or tracing paper, pin the paper to your fabric, and then stitch right through the paper and the fabric together. When you're done, just tear away the paper. This method works well for thick fabrics like felt, which can be tricky to transfer patterns onto any other way.

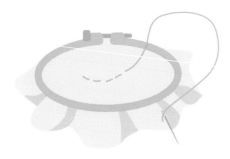

Hoop, Thread, and Stitch!

Now you need to stretch the fabric with the pattern on it onto an embroidery hoop. Place the fabric over the inside frame, and secure the outer frame on top, fitting them together and pulling the fabric tightly between the two.

Next, choose a color of floss, cut a length about 12 inches (30.5 cm) long, and thread your needle. Either tie a knot in the other end of the floss or use an Away Knot if your fabric is light and you're afraid knots will show through (see To Knot or Not?, on the next page).

Now, the fun part—start embroidering! If you're using knots, pull the needle and floss through from the wrong side of your fabric until the knot catches. Then choose a stitch (or use the one called for in the instructions) and follow the lines. When you

finish a line, or when you get down to about 2 inches (5.1 cm) of floss, tie a small knot on the back by slipping your needle under a stitch, looping it, and pulling it tight. Snip off the extra floss and start again. If you are trying to avoid knots, start embroidering but use the steps in To Knot or Not? (on the next page).

to knot or not?

If you're embroidering on thick felt, using knots to secure your floss is fine, but if you want to avoid knots showing through light embroidery cloth (or you're just a neat freak), use the technique called an Away Knot. It's a temporary knot that you start well away from your first stitch and then clip off when once you're done with a section.

1. Make a knot in the end of your floss. Take a small stitch on the back of your fabric well away from where you'll start embroidering, and then bring the needle up through the back of the fabric to the front and start your stitches 1.

2. When you reach the end of the design (or the end of the floss), thread the tail through the stitches on the back of the piece 2, and trim any excess floss from the tail.

3. Cut off the knot, but leave the tail of floss 3.

4. Thread this tail of floss through your needle, and then thread the tail through the beginning stitches on the back of the piece 4. Trim any excess floss from the tail.

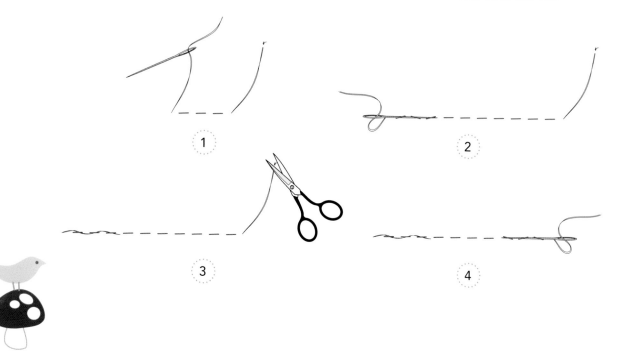

Stitch Reference

Here are the embroidery stitches that are used in the projects in this book.

Straight Stitch

The most basic embroidery stitch, a Straight Stitch can be any length, from a teeny dot to a line about ¼ inch (6 mm) long. Simply pull your needle through from the wrong side of the fabric at A and push it back down at B. To form the Running Stitch, make several Straight Stitches one after another in a line.

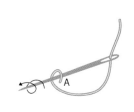

Backstitch

The Backstitch is a simple outlining stitch. Start by making a small stitch backward, from left at A to right at B. Bring your needle back up through the fabric at C, an equal distance ahead of the first stitch, then insert the needle back down at A. Repeat to make each new Backstitch, working backward on the surface and inserting the needle at the end of the previous stitch.

French Knot

French Knots can be tricky at first, but they are well worth taking the time to learn. On their own, they make great dot accents; stitched close together, they can fill an area solidly for an interesting texture. Bring the needle from the wrong side through the fabric at A. Wrap the floss around the tip of the needle in the direction shown, and reinsert the needle at B, right next to A. Pull the floss tight and close to the fabric as you pull the needle back through. Make larger French Knots by wrapping the floss around the needle multiple times.

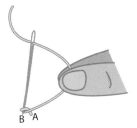
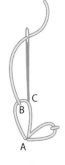

Lazy Daisy Stitch

The Lazy Daisy Stitch is the perfect stitch for making flower petals and leaves. Bring your needle from the wrong side through the fabric at A and put it back down in the same spot, but don't pull the floss all the way through: leave a small loop. Now bring your needle back through the fabric inside the loop at B and back down at C, catching the loop at the top and securing it to the fabric. Repeat this stitch in a circle to make a daisy.

Tying Knots

Some of the projects in this book use knots. It's usually a lot easier to figure out how to tie a specific kind of knot from looking at an image rather than reading about it.

Overhand Knot

This is the simple knot we all make all the time: Make a loop, pass your cord behind and then through the loop, and tighten.

Lark's Head Knot

Fold the cord in half. Place the bend of the cord over another cord (or through a jump ring or the hole in a pendant), bring the free ends of the cord through the loop, and tighten.

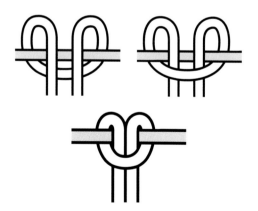

Sliding Knot (or Adjustable Sliding Knot)

Overlap the ends of the cord, right over left, leaving about 4 inches (10.2 cm) of cord on each end ①. Wrap the working cord over the other cord twice ②. Pass the end of the working cord back around itself and then through the wraps ③. Hold the two pieces of cord on the left tight together and pull on the right side of the cord to tighten the knot ④. Then turn the cord over ⑤ and start again to make another sliding knot on the other side ⑥.

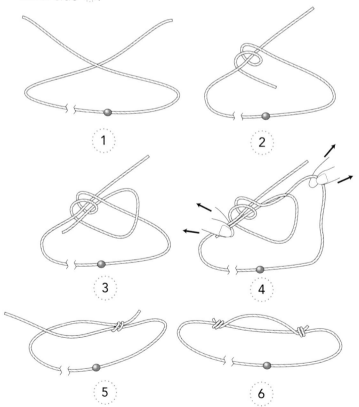

Making Your Own Cabochons and Cameos

The two-part silicone molding putty now available at craft stores and on-line forms a strong, flexible mold you can use to make cabochons and cameos from polymer clay, epoxy clay, or resin. Purchase the kind of molding putty that can be heated in an oven if you are making the cabochon from polymer clay.

Start with vintage cabochons, cameos, or even metal pins from thrifts stores and estate sales. Pry the cabochons or cameos out carefully, use them to make your mold, and then you can glue them back into their original jewelry settings.

Making the Mold

Follow the manufacturer's directions for your specific brand of molding putty, but here are the basic steps to make a mold:

1 Silicone molding putty sets up quickly (usually in about three minutes), so make sure you have the object you're going to use to make the mold (a vintage cameo in this example) clean and ready before you start.

2 Roll equal parts of putty A and putty B into two balls (this is a quick way to visually check that you have equal amounts), making sure that, once combined, you'll have enough molding putty to surround your object with at least an extra ½ inch (1.3 cm) of putty around the sides and the bottom.

3 Knead the two balls together until parts A and B are thoroughly mixed and one solid color instead of marbled, but don't overknead or your putty will start to harden. Shape the putty into one large ball and then flatten it slightly on a craft mat or nonstick surface.

4 Carefully push your object with the design side down into the putty. Let the mold cure undisturbed, with the object still in place, according to the manufacturer's directions (usually 10 to 20 minutes).

5 Once the putty has cured, the object should pop out of the mold easily and cleanly. The mold is now ready to be filled to make your cameo.

Casting the Cameo

Whether you're using epoxy clay or polymer clay (see page 13), the steps to cast in a mold are similar, but the epoxy clay will self-harden and polymer clay will need to be baked.

1 Prepare two balls of clay (one in a lighter color for the profile, one in a darker color for the background) following the manufacturer's directions.

2 Fill just the profile section of the mold with the lighter color clay. Gently swipe a fingertip across the top of the clay, going from the outside toward the center, to smooth the top and remove any clay from outside the profile part of the cavity. The neater the edges of your clay, the crisper your cameo image will be.

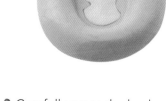

3 Carefully press the background clay on top of the clay in the profile, filling to the top of the mold. Again smooth from the outside edges into the center of the clay to smooth the surface and remove any excess clay from the top of the mold.

4 For epoxy clay, just set the mold aside and let it cure following the manufacturer's directions. For polymer clay, bake it right in the mold following the manufacturer's directions. Put the mold on a cookie sheet, and use oven mitts—the mold will get hot!

5 Once cured or baked and cooled, your cameo should pop right out of the mold. Use sandpaper, an emery board, or a file to smooth the edges of the cameo if needed, but for best results, wait at least 24 hours before doing so.

tip

- If you add colorant to resin, you can cast cabochons with it, too. See page 107 for information on working with resin.

Needle Felting

You needle felt by using a needle-felting needle to poke wool roving (cotton-candy-like carded wool) repeatedly to compress it and shape it into three-dimensional forms. As the felting needle goes in and out of the felt, its tiny barbs catch and drop the wool fibers, tangling and enmeshing the layers to create a firm shape.

The technique is easy to learn, and a simple ball shape is a good place to start. Begin by either rolling a small wad of wool between your palms to form a ball or by rolling the wool into a snake shape and then rolling that up into a tight spiral. Set the ball of wool on a piece of foam 2 inches (5.1 cm)

thick (to protect your fingers and your surface!) and then start poking. Just insert the felting needle down into the felt and then withdraw it from the same hole in a straight up-and-down motion—the straighter, the better. Watch your fingers: the needle is painfully sharp!

Move around as you work to create a firm, even shape. If your ball firms up but is now too small, add a bit of wool and poke on. Squeeze the ball gently; if you feel soft spots, felt that area more, adding a little more wool if needed.

To attach two felted shapes together, simply hold them against each other and needle felt by poking back and forth from one to the other repeatedly, as shown in the illustration.

Making Shrink-Plastic Jewelry

The steps for using shrink plastic to make jewelry are really quite simple. The Hedgehog Necklace (page 60) was made from special inkjet shrink plastic that you can print directly onto. (Use an inkjet printer—don't try this with a laser printer or you can damage your printer!) Baking temperatures vary for different types and brands of shrink plastic, so always follow the manufacturer's directions.

1 Sand the plastic (if it isn't the inkjet or pre-roughened kind).

2 Draw, trace, or photocopy a design onto the plastic. Cut the design out.

3 Use a hole punch to punch any necessary holes in the plastic so you can add findings once it's shrunk.

4 Preheat your oven to the temperature recommended for your shrink plastic. (Don't insert cardboard or paper into an oven or toaster oven as it's preheating, because some ovens have temperature spikes while preheating that are high enough to set the cardboard or paper on fire.)

5 Place your unbaked item on a small piece of cardboard or parchment paper on a flat baking sheet. If the piece is long, you can add a piece of parchment paper on top—shrink plastic initially curls as it heats up, and the paper will keep the curling plastic from sticking to itself.

6 Once your piece has flattened back down (usually in about three minutes), it's done.

7 Using an oven mitt or gloves, carefully remove the baking sheet from the oven, place it on a heat-resistant surface, and press down slightly on the warm piece using a smooth hardcover book or other object to completely flatten it.

8 Your piece will not be waterproof, so once it has cooled, seal it with an acrylic sealer, spray sealer, liquid dimensional gloss, or even clear fingernail polish.

9 Add findings to make your jewelry.

tip

- Shrink plastic sold for crafts is safe even when heated beyond recommended temperatures, but because you don't know for certain whether all the mediums you use to decorate your plastic are nontoxic, use separate baking equipment for it. And it does release fumes, so open a window before you start. If you're sensitive to fumes, you can purchase a dedicated toaster oven from a thrift shop to use outside with an outdoor extension cord (in dry weather, of course).

Adding Jump Rings

Jump rings allow you to make quick and easy connections between jewelry parts. If you open or close a jump ring incorrectly by pulling the ends apart or together, you'll distort its shape and weaken the link. Instead, use two pairs of pliers to grasp each end of the jump ring. Then pull one side toward you and the other side away from you on the same plane 1 . Open the jump ring only as wide as necessary to insert the objects being joined. To close the jump ring, simply reverse the process by twisting the ends back together.

Making a Simple Loop

A simple loop is as simple to make as its name.

1 As shown in 2 , use chain-nose pliers to bend the end of the wire 90° to make a right angle, leaving enough wire at the end to make a loop.

2 Using round-nose pliers, grasp the wire close to the bend of the angle, then roll the pliers to shape the loop 3 . Use flush wire cutters to trim any excess wire.

3 The finished loop is ready for attachment 4 . Once it's in place, gently squeeze the loop with pliers to secure it.

Making a Simple Loop Link

To make a bead loop link 5 , just make a simple loop, add a bead or beads to the wire, and then make another simple loop.

Making a Wrapped Loop

As shown in 6 , the wrapped loop is a variation of the simple loop just described. Use an extra length of wire for the 90° bend. Once you've made the loop, reposition the pliers so that the lower jaw is inside it. Using your other hand and, keeping the wire at a right angle as you work, wrap the wire tail around the neck of the wire two or three times. Cut the wire, and then tuck in the end close to the remaining length.

Making a Wrapped Loop Link

To make a wrapped bead loop link 7 , just make a wrapped loop, add a bead or beads to the wire, and then make another wrapped loop.

Projects

Designer Aimee Ray

Woodland Friends Necklaces

Air-drying paper clay makes these necklaces a cinch to make and nice and light to wear.

materials
(to make the Owl)

- Small amount of air-drying paper clay
- 1 silver headpin, 2 inches (5.1 cm) long
- White craft glue (optional)
- Watercolor or acrylic paints
- Clear acrylic varnish
- 18-inch (45.7cm) length of silver ball chain

tools

- Flush wire cutters
- Tiny brushes
- Chain-nose or needle-nose pliers
- Round-nose pliers

1 Form the clay into a small mound about ½ inch (1.3 cm) tall, rounded on the top and flat on the bottom; pull a small point at the bottom for the tail feathers. (For the gnome, make a cylinder shape with a pointed top and a flat bottom. For the fox, make a cylinder shape with two points at the top for ears and a flat bottom.) Push the headpin through it from the bottom up and allow it to dry thoroughly.

2 Clip the top off of the headpin, leaving ½ inch (1.3 cm), and bend the remaining wire into a simple loop (see page 28). You may need to apply a bit of glue to the bottom of the headpin to keep it in place.

3 Paint your owl design. Begin with an arch on the front and add a little pointed beak in the top center. Paint a color around the back and sides of the arch. Next, add tiny details like eyes and lines for feathers and wings.

4 When the paint is dry, coat the owl with the clear acrylic varnish. Allow to dry thoroughly.

5 Slip the silver ball chain through the loop.

Embroidered Felt Pin

This felt pin is so cute it can easily be the focal point of an outfit. With a few stitches, you have an instant one-of-a-kind piece.

1 Use the templates to trace circles A, B, and C onto the felt with the disappearing fabric marker.

2 Cut one circle A and one circle C from the felt with the pinking shears.

3 Cut one circle B from the felt with the scissors.

4 Trace the design onto tissue paper and pin the paper to the smaller pinked felt circle.

5 Embroider the design with floss colors and stitches as indicated (see next page), but do not stitch the outer circle of broken lines yet.

6 Center the embroidered circle onto the large pinked circle. Use the Straight Stitch (page 22) or Running Stitch (page 22) and light turquoise floss to attach the two pinked circles, leaving a small opening before completing stitched the circle. Remove the tissue paper.

7 Stuff a small amount of cotton fill into the opening and then stitch to complete the circle.

8 Cut one circle D from stiff cardboard.

materials

- Templates (page 122)
- Aqua blue felt
- Embroidery floss in khaki, medium gray, cream, and light turquoise*
- Cotton fill
- Stiff cardboard
- Fabric glue
- 1 bar pin
- * Sandie used DMC embroidery floss colors 833, 645, 3866, and 598.

tools

- Pinking shears
- Scissors
- Tissue paper
- Straight pins
- Large embroidery needle

back

9 Using fabric glue, center and attach the cardboard circle to the back of the large pinked circle of felt.

10 Sew the bar pin to the remaining circle of felt.

11 Glue the assemblage onto the cardboard to form the back of the pin.

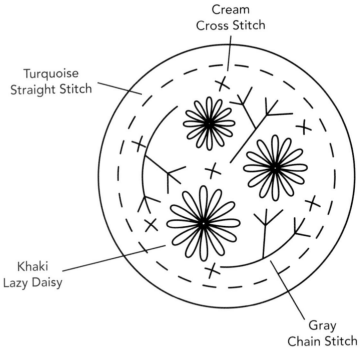

Cream
Cross Stitch

Turquoise
Straight Stitch

Khaki
Lazy Daisy

Gray
Chain Stitch

Wrapped Bead Bracelet

Designer *Jennifer M. Burgess*

Wrapped Bead Bracelet

Sure you can buy one of these super popular wrapped bracelets, but with bamboo cord, beads, a metal button, and a few basic knots, you can make your very own in the colors of your choice.

materials

- 4¼-yard (3.9 m) length of 1-mm bamboo cord in shifting neutral colors
- 1 flower-shaped metal button with shank, ⅝ to ¾ inch (1.6 to 1.9 cm)
- 5-yard (4.6 m) length of FireLine bead thread, 6-pound test
- 62 earth-toned round beads, 8 mm
- Jewelry adhesive
- 4 dark gray hematite size 8° seed beads

tools

- Beading needle, size 12
- Clipboard

Note: This technique seems tricky at first, but once you get wrapping, you'll suddenly "get it" and see how easy it is. Refer to the illustration as you go (the doubled bamboo cord used in the project is shown as single in the illustration for simplicity's sake).

1 Double the bamboo cord. Pass the doubled cord through the button's shank and center the button on the length of cord. Cut the fold so you now have four cord ends. With all ends of the cord gathered, make a loose Overhand Knot (page 23) close to the button—but don't pull tight.

2 Thread the beading needle with the FireLine; center the needle and tie an Overhand Knot with both ends of the FireLine.

3 Immediately under the button but above the loose cord knot, on one side of the cording, attach the FireLine with a Lark's Head Knot (page 23). To strengthen this attachment, do one or two more Lark's Head Knots and/or a couple of Overhand Knots. When satisfied, pass the needle through the cord's loose knot; tighten the knot.

4 Use the clipboard to secure the button in place. Separate the cords into left- and right-hand sides and then proceed as follows:

- Bring the beading needle and FireLine underneath the left cord and thread one 8-mm round bead onto the FireLine.

- Scoot the bead down the Fireline until it presses against the left cord, then secure it with your fingers between both of the cords.

- Bring the needle and FireLine under and then over the right cord, pass the needle through the same bead to the left and then over the top of the left cord, tugging slightly to pick up any slack in the thread.

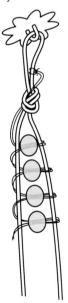

(continued on page 38)

Wrapped Bead Bracelet

5 Repeat step 4 with each bead for the desired length of the bracelet, leaving at least 6 inches (15.2 cm) of cording to accommodate the knotting.

6 With the last bead in place, use the needle to pass the FireLine back and forth inside the bead two to four times, wrapping the thread around the cording each time. You may also want to add an Overhand Knot or two on either side.

7 Tie an Overhand Knot with all the cording close to the last bead. Do not tighten.

8 To secure the FireLine further, pass the needle through the loose knot tied in step 7. Tighten the cording knot and tie an Overhand Knot twice in the FireLine close to the cording knot. Dab the FireLine knot with a small amount of jewelry adhesive.

9 With all of the cord ends, tie another loose Overhand Knot in the cording approximately ½ inch (1.3 cm) from the first knot. Pass the button halfway through the space between the two knots to size the closure; tighten the Overhand Knot. You may add another closure space for adjustability by tying more Overhand Knots; otherwise, proceed to step 10.

10 Add a size 8° seed bead to each end of cording and tie an Overhand Knot on each cord to secure. Trim the cording to the preferred length.

Felt Circle Rings

Designer Paola Benenati

materials

- White masking tape
- 2 different colored pieces of felt, at least ¾ x ¾ inch (1.9 x 1.9 cm)
- 1 ring blank with round bezel, at least ½ inch (1.3 cm) in diameter
- White school glue

tools

- Pencil
- Small, sharp scissors
- ¼-inch (6 mm) hole punch (size will depend on size of the bezel in your ring blank; see step 3)
- Sewing needle (optional, see Tip)

Felt Circle Rings

Possible color combinations are endless with these simple and striking felt rings.

1 Put a piece of masking tape on one piece of felt and draw a circle on the tape by tracing around the bezel.

2 With a pair of sharp scissors, cut out the circle of felt by cutting about ¹⁄₁₆ inch (1.6 mm) inside the traced line. Make sure the cut felt fits inside the bezel.

3 Mark the center of the cut circle with the pencil and make a hole with the hole punch. (You can fold the circle into quarters to find the exact midpoint.)

4 Use the hole punch to cut out another circle from the other felt color.

5 Remove the masking tape from the larger circle and place the smaller felt circle inside the punched-out hole

6 Cover the wrong side of both pieces of felt with a small amount of glue and place them on the base of the ring.

7 Press the felt lightly with your finger so that the surface is smooth and adhered to the ring. Let it dry.

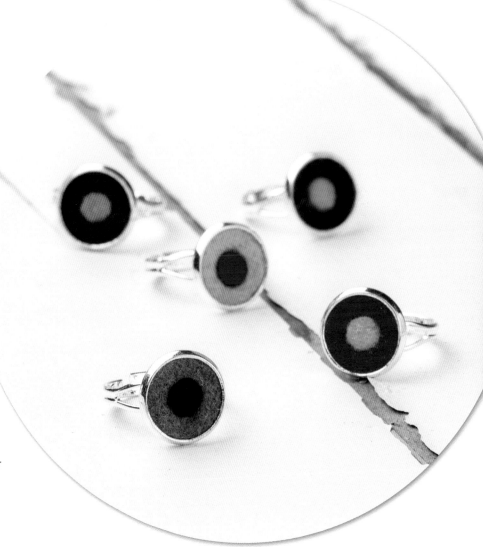

tip

- If any felt threads are poking up, use a sewing needle to push them back down.

Warm Beach Hoops

These delicate beaded hoops look intricate, but the technique is really just a matter of wrap, insert bead, wrap, insert bead…

materials

- 30-inch (76.2 cm) length of 24-gauge gold craft wire
- 40 rondelles (chalcedony or any other gemstone), 3.5 mm
- 2 gold-plated earrings hoops, 1 inch (2.5 cm) in diameter

tools

- Flush wire cutters
- Flat-nose pliers

1 Using the flush wire cutters, cut the craft wire in half so you have two 15-inch (38.1 cm) pieces.

2 Arrange 20 rondelles on a flat surface based on their colors or other desired arrangement.

3 Wrap the wire four times around the earring hoop, starting at the looped end of the hoop.

4 Insert the first rondelle. When it touches the hoop, hold it in position using your index finger and thumb and, with your other hand, twist the wire around the hoop one or two times. Make sure the bead doesn't come loose.

5 Repeat the same process until you wrap all 20 rondelles on one hoop, and as you wrap the rondelles, push them close to each other for a neat look.

6 When you've finished wrapping all the rondelles, secure the wire by making four more wraps, ending ⅝ inch (1.6 cm) from the end of the hoop. Trim away the excess wire and bend the cut end with flat-nose pliers so that it doesn't stick out.

7 Repeat steps 2 through 6 to make the second earring.

Designer Aimee Ray

Felted Terrarium Necklace

No watering needed for this needle-felted terrarium. But you may want to leave it open at night so fairies can come in and play.

1 To start making the tiny mushroom, needle-felt a disk ½ inch (1.3 cm) wide in pink wool roving for the cap, and felt three tiny spots of white wool on top. See page 26 for more on needle-felting.

2 Make a cylinder ½ inch (1.3 cm) long from white wool roving, and attach it to the bottom of the mushroom cap ⊙.

3 Felt the mushroom stem to the circle of light green felt. Add moss around the base of the mushroom with the green roving ②.

See page 26 for more on needle-felting.

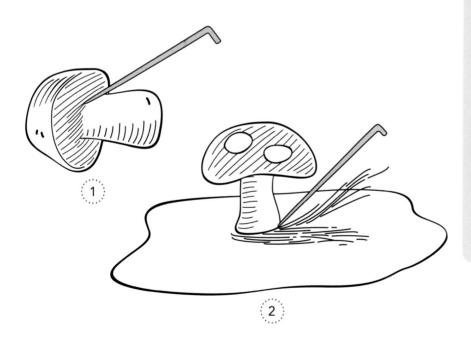

materials

- Wool roving in pink, white, and moss green
- 1 circle of light green felt, 1⅛ inches (2.9 cm) in diameter
- Scrap of moss green felt
- Embroidery floss in pale green, pink, and dark pink*
- White school glue
- Round, clear dome charm, 1¼ x 2 inches (3.2 x 5.1 cm) (available online)
- 1 silver jump ring, 6 mm
- 24-inch (61 cm) length of silver chain with clasp

  * Aimee used DMC embroidery floss in colors 3348, 761, and 760.

tools

- Needle-felting needle and foam
- Embroidery scissors or other small, sharp scissors
- Embroidery needle
- 2 pairs of chain-nose pliers

Felted Terrarium Necklace

4. Cut three tiny leaves from the moss green felt. Using two or three strands of green embroidery floss, stitch them in place around the mushroom.

5. Embroider a pink flower using the Lazy Daisy Stitch (page 22) on the base and add tiny dark pink French Knots (page 22).

6. Glue the felt circle to the base of the dome and attach the dome over it.

7. Use the jump ring to attach the loop at the top of the pendant to the chain.

Feather Earrings

These rooster feather earrings make a big impact and they're comfortable to wear—after all, they're light as feathers.

Designer Sonya Fabricant

Feather Earrings

materials

- 6 Chinese saddle hackle rooster feathers in white (see Note)
- 4 cape rooster feathers in ginger grizzly
- 2 Chinese saddle hackle rooster feathers in blue
- Jewelry adhesive
- 2 gold spring-coil cord ends, with ³⁄₃₂-inch (2.4 mm) opening
- 2 gold earring hoops, ¾ inch (1.9 cm) in diameter

tools

- Scissors
- Chain-nose pliers

NOTE: Fly-fishing shops are a good place to find a large selection of rooster feathers.

1 Select a white feather. Trim it down to 3 inches (7.6 cm) with the scissors, then use your fingers to strip ⅛ inch (3 mm) of plumage from the top of the feather.

2 Dab a tiny amount of jewelry adhesive on this stripped area and slip it into the cord end. Press it against the back of the spring so that the front of the feather faces up.

3 Select a long ginger feather and strip about ⅛ inch (3 mm) of plumage from the top.

4 Dab adhesive onto the stripped area and lay it on top of the white feather in the cord end.

5 Trim, strip, and glue the rest of the feathers. Follow the long ginger feather with another white feather, followed by a blue feather, followed by a white feather. Lay a slender ginger feather on the very top. Let dry completely.

6 Thread the earring hoop through the loop of the cord end. With the pliers, bend the flush end of the earring hoop up at a 90° angle so that it hooks into the small loop on the other end of the hoop.

7 Repeat these steps to make a second earring.

Map Rings

Epoxy clay — which hardens without baking or firing — and simple image transfer are the keys to these map rings.

1 Trim the photocopy to match the size of your ring's bezel with a little overlap.

tip

- This project uses a copyrighted image with permission. Remember to only use copyright-free images for any jewelry that you are selling. Also, the transferred image will be the reverse of the original image, so if orientation is important, scan and flip the image on your computer. Laser or toner-based printer copies usually work best for image transfer. If you only have access to an inkjet printer, test an image from it on a scrap piece of epoxy clay first.

2 Either wear disposable gloves or apply hand cream or olive oil to your hands so the epoxy clay won't stick. Mix two equal-size balls of part A and part B of the white epoxy clay (the amount will depend on the size of your ring's bezel). Mix the two balls together, following the manufacturer's instructions, and roll into one ball.

3 Push the ball of mixed epoxy clay down into the ring bezel, stretching the clay out and making sure to push the clay into the corners of the bezel. Work until the bezel cavity is full and the surface is even. Stretching the clay as opposed to compressing it to fill the bezel will leave the clay tackier, and it will take the transfer better.

materials

- Small color photocopy of image (see Tip)
- Hand cream, olive oil, or disposable gloves
- White epoxy clay
- Ring blank with bezel

tools

- Scissors
- Spoon
- Bowl of room-temperature water

Map Rings

4 Place the color photocopy in the desired position face down onto the freshly mixed clay in the bezel.

5 Use the back of the spoon to burnish the color photocopy to the clay. Set the piece aside and let it cure for at least three to four hours, if not overnight.

6 After the clay has cured, use your fingers to dab the room-temperature water liberally onto the back of the photocopy on top of the clay and then allow it to sit for five minutes.

7 Dab more water on the paper and start rubbing a finger over the back of the copy, removing the wet paper. The color image will be left behind on the clay as the paper is removed. Continue adding water and rubbing until all the paper is removed. Dry any remaining moisture off the clay. Let the clay dry for 24 hours before wearing the ring.

Felted Acorn Necklace

Designer Donni Webber

materials

- Acorn cap
- ¾ inch (1.9 cm) length of ribbon, ¹⁄₁₆ inch (1.6 mm) wide
- White school glue
- Blue wool roving
- Oval jump ring
- Metal leaf charm
- Necklace chain

tools

- Old toothbrush
- Baking dish
- Oven
- Drill with a small drill bit
- Ruler
- Tweezers
- Needle-felting needle and foam
- 2 pairs of flat-nose pliers

NOTE: If you're new to needle felting, read the information on page 26.

Felted Acorn Necklace

The simple shape of this felted acorn makes it an ideal project for beginning needle-felters.

1 Clean off the acorn cap by brushing it softly with an old toothbrush. Set it in a baking dish and put it in the oven at a low temperature (200°F [93°C]) for 30 minutes. This low heat will kill any bugs or bug eggs living inside the cap. Set the acorn cap aside to cool.

2 Use the drill to make a small hole about ¹⁄₁₆ inch (1.6 mm) below the woody stem of the acorn cap. Fold the ¾-inch (1.9 cm) piece of ribbon in half crosswise and use the tweezers to thread the folded end of the ribbon through the hole in the acorn cap from the inside. Use a little glue to secure the cut ends of the ribbon in place inside the acorn cap. Allow the glue to dry completely.

3 To make the colorful wool "acorn" to go inside the acorn cap, pull off a tuft of blue wool roving about three times as large as you want your finished ball to be. Roll it in your hands as if you were rolling a ball of dough, gently at first and then apply more pressure as you feel the wool ball in your hands firm up a little. Use the needle-felting needle and mat to needle felt all around the outside of the wool ball. As you needle felt, you will see the ball start to firm up and become more compact in size. Keep needle felting it evenly until the wool ball is smooth, round, and the correct size to fit into the acorn cap.

4 Secure the blue wool ball in the acorn cap with a little glue and allow it to dry completely.

5 Open the jump ring with two pairs of flat-nose pliers and hook it through the small ribbon loop on the outside of the acorn cap and the metal leaf charm. Close the jump ring and thread the chain through it.

Designer *Kathy Sheldon*

Cabochon Hairpins

Making your own cabochons from molds is not just easy — it's also addictive! Buy some hairpin findings and turn your homemade cabs into hair accessories.

1 Follow the instructions on page 24 to use the two-part silicone molding putty to make a mold from your cabochon, cameo, or pin.

2 Follow the instructions on page 25 to use the polymer clay or epoxy clay to make a cameo or cabochon from your mold. For translucent cabochons, try using two-part resin with colorant instead. See page 107 for more on resin.

3 Apply jewelry adhesive to the back of the cameo or cabochon, center the piece over the blank on the hairpin finding, and press to adhere. Allow the glue to dry thoroughly.

materials

- Two-part silicone molding putty
- Vintage cabochons, cameos, metal pins, and other objects to mold (see Note)
- Polymer clay or epoxy clay in multiple colors, or two-part resin and colorant
- Jewelry adhesive
- Hairpin findings

tools

- Nonstick work surface
- Oven
- Cardboard

NOTE: It's easy to find vintage cameos and costume jewelry at yard sales and in thrift shops. Take them apart to get pieces you can use to make molds.

Designer Aimee Ray

Fabric Scrap Necklaces

Don't toss the scraps from your last sewing project — make these sweet necklaces instead.

materials

- Templates (page 122)
- Scraps of brown, green, and tan fabric
- Embroidery floss in brown, pale green, and tan*
- Fabric glue (optional)
- 24-inch (61 cm) length of green or tan ribbon, ⅛ inch (3 mm) wide

  * Aimee used DMC embroidery floss colors 869, 3348, and 422.

tools

- Supplies to transfer the template design (see page 20)
- Embroidery needle
- Fabric scissors

1 Follow the instructions on page 20 to transfer the template design of your choice onto a small piece of fabric. Embroider it as indicated on the template and cut it out, leaving a ¼-inch (6 mm) border around the edge.

2 Cut a piece of fabric in a different color, ¼ inch (6 mm) larger than the embroidered piece. Stitch the embroidered piece onto the background using the Running Stitch (page 22), or glue it on using fabric glue.

3 Cut a third piece of fabric the same size and shape as the background piece. Align it with the front section and use a Running Stitch around the edge to hold them together.

4 With embroidery floss, stitch four same-size loops at the top of the fabric charm and slide it onto the length of ribbon. Tie the ribbon in a bow around your neck to the desired length.

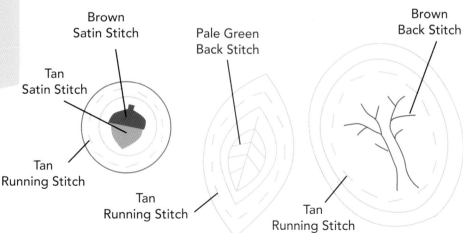

Brown Satin Stitch

Tan Satin Stitch

Tan Running Stitch

Pale Green Back Stitch

Tan Running Stitch

Brown Back Stitch

Tan Running Stitch

Hedgehog Shrink Plastic Necklace

Inkjet shrink plastic allows you to print this sweet hedgehog image right onto the plastic and then shrink it down into the perfect pendant.

 Scan the hedgehog template into a document on your computer.

tip

- If you have an inkjet printer/copier, you can copy the image right onto the shrink plastic instead of scanning it into your computer and then printing, but the scanning method makes it easier to print multiple images onto a sheet of inkjet plastic at once so you don't waste material.

Because baking makes the image's color darken and intensify as the piece shrinks, this template has already been lightened and enlarged, but you may still want to print the image on a piece of paper first to test for positioning and color. When printing an image, always make it two to three times larger and about 50 percent lighter than your desired final piece.

materials

- Template (page 123)
- White inkjet shrink plastic (See note)
- Computer (optional, see Tip)
- Inkjet printer (see note)
- Scissors
- Small curved scissors
- ¼ inch (6 mm) hole punch
- Oven or toaster oven
- Parchment paper
- Baking sheet
- Potholder or oven mitt
- Flattener (heavy smooth object such as a book)
- Matte acrylic spray sealer
- 24-inch (61 cm) length of leather cord
- Jump ring

tools

- Two pairs chain-nose pliers

NOTE: Inkjet shrink plastic is available both online and in many craft stores. Do not try to use this type of shrink plastic in a laser printer—it can melt and ruin your printer. See pages 14 and 27 for more on shrink plastic.

Hedgehog Shrink Plastic Necklace

2 Remove any paper from your printer's tray and feed the inkjet sheet through the printer just as you would paper. If only one side of the shrink plastic is printable, the manufacturer's instructions should explain how to tell which side it is. (If you're uncertain which side of the sheet your printer prints on, run a test sheet of paper through with an X drawn on it.)

3 Handling the printed inkjet sheet plastic carefully by its edges, place it on a flat surface to dry. Drying time will vary by shrink plastic brand and the amount of ink in the image.

4 Use the scissors to cut out the image (the small curved scissors will be helpful when cutting the scalloped edges). Turn the shrink plastic rather than the scissors, for the smoothest cut.

5 Use the ¼-inch (6 mm) hole punch to make a hole in each scalloped edge.

6 Follow the instructions on page 27 to bake the hedgehog. (That doesn't sound very good, does it?) Once it has completely shrunk, remove it from the oven and flatten the piece with a heavy smooth object, such as a book, while it is still warm, then allow it to cool completely.

7 Seal the piece by spraying it lightly with the matte acrylic spray sealer. Let it dry completely.

8 Follow the instructions on page 23 to make a sliding knot necklace from the leather cord.

9 Use the jump ring to attach the hedgehog pendant to the cord.

Super Simple Flower Posts

These self-stick plastic flower cabochons were in the scrapbooking section of a craft store.

materials

- 2 self-stick flower cabochons
- Jewelry adhesive
- 2 earring posts and backs

tool

- Sandpaper (optional, see Tip)

1 Remove the self-stick goop from the back of each flower.

2 Apply jewelry adhesive to the back of each post.

3 Attach one flower to each post and it let dry completely.

Designer *Kathy Sheldon*

tip

- For a super tight bond, sand the flat surface of each earring post and the back of each plastic flower cabochon lightly with sandpaper, clean, and then apply the jewelry adhesive.

Button Blossom Earrings

This project shows how felt, floss, and buttons
make a winning combination.

Designer **Melissa Davison**

1. Trace the templates onto the thin cardboard, cut them out, and then use the cardboard templates to trace four large ovals onto the pink felt and two small ovals onto the ecru felt.

2. Cut out each felt oval, being careful to stay just inside the tracing lines.

3. Center each ecru oval onto one pink oval. Thread the needle with three plies of knotted pink floss. Use a medium-length Straight Stitch (page 22) to attach the ecru ovals to the pink ovals, stitching close to the edge.

4. With the pink floss, sew each flower button to the center of an ecru oval, close to the top. Using the green floss, make three long Straight Stitches down the center of the ecru oval to form the stem, beginning the top stitch just underneath the flower button. Make a single Lazy Daisy Stitch (page 22) at the left and right of the center of the stem to form two leaves. Repeat for the second ecru oval.

5. Match the front and back pink oval pieces. With three plies of ecru floss, attach the front and back of both earrings with a medium-length Straight Stitch close to the edge of the pink ovals.

6. To form a loop to attach the oval to a jump ring, thread the needle with a small length of three plies of pink floss and knot the end. Trim the remaining floss close to the knot. Insert the needle between the two pink ovals at the center top, bringing the needle out on the wrong side about 3/16 inch (5 mm) from the edge of the circle. Pull until the knot catches snugly between the two circles so that it is completely hidden. Bring the needle back around to the front piece, pulling it back through next to the knot. Repeat two more times until you have a solid loop of floss at the center top of the pink oval. Finish off the floss by hiding a few tiny stitches beneath the loop. Repeat for the second earring.

7. Open a small jump ring and insert one end through all the strands of the floss loop on the top of an oval. Insert the opposite open end of the jump ring into the loop of the earring hook and twist the ring back together. Repeat with the second earring.

materials

- Templates (page 123)
- Thin cardboard for pattern tracing
- Hot pink wool felt
- Ecru wool felt
- Embroidery floss in pink, green, and ecru*
- 2 pink flower-shaped buttons
- 2 small silver jump rings
- 2 silver earring hooks

* Melissa used DMC embroidery floss colors 600, 703, and ecru.

tools

- Fabric pen or disappearing fabric marker
- Scissors
- Embroidery needle, size 5
- 2 pairs of chain-nose pliers

Garden Party Bracelet and Earrings

Cabochons and lace-edge settings are a combination that make jewelry construction sweet and simple.

Make the Cabochon Settings

1 Apply the jewelry adhesive evenly to the flat back of one floral decal cabochon and place it in one lace-edge cup setting. Repeat with the remaining floral decal cabochons and lace-edge cup settings. Set aside to dry completely.

2 Apply the jewelry adhesive evenly to the flat back of one dahlia cabochon and place it in one round lace-edge setting. Repeat with remaining dahlias and round lace-edge settings. Set aside to dry completely.

Make the Bracelet

1 Open a jump ring. Catch one loop of a dahlia setting and then one loop of a floral cabochon setting in it. Close the jump ring.

Designer *Kathy Sheldon*

materials

- Jewelry adhesive
- 6 floral decal cabochons, 13 x 18 mm
- 6 brass lace-edge cup settings, 13 x 18 mm (the kind with two loops down)
- 4 ivory dahlia cabochons, 10 mm
- 4 brass round lace-edge settings, 10 mm
- 11 gold jump rings, 5 mm
- Gold toggle clasp set
- 2 light blue glass teardrop stones in loop settings
- 2 gold ear wires

tools

- 2 pairs of chain-nose pliers

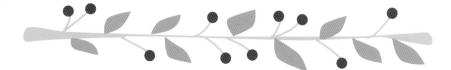

Garden Party Bracelet and Earrings

2. Continue adding dahlia settings and floral decal cabochon settings with jump rings until the piece is 7 inches (17.8 cm) in length (adjust for larger or smaller wrists, leaving room for your clasp).

3. Use a jump ring to attach each end of your clasp set to the assemblage.

Make the Earrings

1. Open a jump ring. Hook it through the bottom loop of a floral decal cabochon setting and the loop of one light blue glass teardrop. Close the jump ring. Repeat for the second earring.

2. Open the loop of one of the ear wires. Catch the top loop of one floral decal cabochon setting in it, then close it. Repeat for the second ear wire.

back

Lantern Earrings

Designer Nathalie Mornu

Lantern Earrings

In this project, it's all about the proportion of the beads to each other. You'll probably spend less time putting together these delicate earrings than you will shopping for the perfect beads to use.

materials

- 3 inches (7.6 cm) of fine brass chain
- 2 brass jump rings, 4 mm
- 2 brass jump rings, 7 mm
- 2 fancy brass beads with built-in loops, 1 cm (see Tip)
- 4 filigree bead caps, 7 mm
- 2 white glass beads, 8 mm
- 2 brass eye pins, 2 inches (5.1 cm) long
- 2 brass ear wires

tools

- Flush wire cutters
- 2 pairs of chain-nose pliers
- Round-nose pliers

tip

- All the different types of brass beads on the market can make a project really special. The twists used in the project shown look like Chinese lanterns and give it an exotic flair. Filigree beads embedded with crystals, right, will lend your earrings an Edwardian air.

1 Cut a piece of brass chain 1⅛ inches (2.9 cm) long. Count how many links it has, cut a second piece of chain with that same number of links in it, and set one of the pieces aside to use later when making the second earring.

2 Open one of the 4-mm jump rings. Slide on one end of a piece of chain, as well as one of the brass beads (using its built-in loop), then close the jump ring. Set aside.

3 Slide a bead cap, a white bead, and another bead cap onto an eye pin. Form a loop to keep the beads on the wire. This element is called a *bead loop*.

4 Open the loop on one of the ear wires. Catch either one of the loops in the bead loop in it, then close it.

5 Open a 7-mm jump ring. Catch the unused loop of the bead loop in it, and also the unused loop in the brass bead. One earring made!

6 Repeat steps 2 through 5 to make the other earring, using the remaining piece of chain set aside in step 1.

Designer *Melissa Davison*

Retro Button Bracelet

Circles of felt, cheerful buttons, and colorful floss add up to a bracelet that will make you feel happy every time you wear it!

1. Trace the circle template patterns directly onto the felt in the following colors and sizes: two large blue, two large orange, one small orange, two large yellow, one small yellow, two large red, two large green, and one small green.

2. Cut out each felt circle, being careful to stay just inside the tracing lines.

3. With three knotted plies of the white floss, stitch the two large buttons to the centers of a large orange circle and a large red circle. Finish with a knot on the wrong side.

4. With three knotted plies of the blue floss, use a medium-length Straight Stitch (page 22) to attach another orange circle (the back) to the front orange circle with the button. Finish with a few tiny hidden stitches on the wrong side. Do the same for the red circles using the yellow floss.

5. With the white floss, stitch the three small buttons to the small yellow, green, and orange circles.

6. Center the small yellow circle on one large blue circle. With the blue floss, join the yellow and blue circles with a ring of French Knots (page 22), spacing them about 3/16 inch (5 mm) apart. Do the same for the small green circle and the large yellow circle using yellow floss, and with the small orange circle and the large green circle using green floss.

7. Attach the remaining large blue circle to the back of the joined blue and yellow circles with a medium-length Straight Stitch using the yellow floss. Do the same for the large yellow circle and the

materials

- Templates (page 122)
- Wool felt in five colors: navy blue, orange, yellow, red, and green
- Embroidery floss in white, blue, yellow, green, orange, and red*
- 2 buttons, ¾ inch (19 mm) in diameter
- 3 buttons, 7/16 inch (11 mm) in diameter
- 6 small oval brass jump rings
- 1 brass clasp

  * Melissa used DMC embroidery floss in colors white, 796, 444, 909, 721, and 666

tools

- Disappearing fabric marker
- Scissors
- Embroidery needle
- 2 pairs of chain-nose pliers

small green circle using the green floss, and the large green circle and the small orange circle using the orange floss.

8. Thread the needle with a small length of three plies of blue thread and knot the end. Trim the remaining thread close to the knot. Insert the needle between the two large blue circles, bringing the needle out on the back circle about 3/16 inch (5 mm) from the edge of the circle, pulling until the knot catches snugly between the two circles so that it is completely hidden. Bring the needle back around to the original insertion point, pulling it back through next to the knot. Repeat two more times until you have a solid loop of thread on the back circle only. Insert the needle into the back circle next to the loop and pull it out at the opposite side of the circle, keeping the needle between the two circles. Stitch a second loop directly opposite the first on the other side of the circle. Finish off the thread by hiding a few tiny stitches beneath the second loop. Make two thread loops for each large circle piece using matching thread.

9. Open a small jump ring using two pairs of pliers and insert one end through all the strands of a thread loop on the blue circle. Insert the opposite open end of the jump ring into the thread loop of the orange circle and twist the ring back together. Repeat with all the thread loops until each of the five pieces is joined together, alternating the large and small button pieces.

10. Attach a jump ring to each of the two bracelet ends using the remaining thread loops. Attach the jump ring to each end of the clasp.

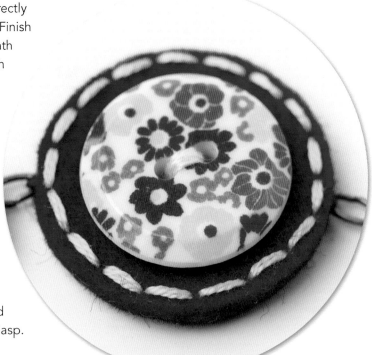

back

*Butterfly
Specimen Locket*

Designer *Morgan Shooter*

Butterfly Specimen Locket

You don't need a butterfly net to capture the lovely specimens in this locket—a photocopier will work just fine.

materials

- Templates (page 123)
- Clear spray sealer
- Hinged box pendant
- Scrap of cream-colored, textured paper (for background)
- Cyanoacrylate glue
- Chain with clasp

tools

- Color photocopier
- Small scissors or craft knife
- Ruler
- Pencil
- Toothpick
- Tweezers

1 Make a color photocopy of the template's butterfly images, adjusting the size if needed to fit inside the pendant—but don't cut the butterflies out yet! Using the clear spray sealer, give each side of the paper several light coats, letting the sealer dry thoroughly between coats.

2 Once the butterfly images are sealed and completely dry, use the small scissors or craft knife to cut each one out very carefully. Fold each butterfly lengthwise down the center of its body.

3 To make the background for the butterflies, measure the inside dimensions of the hinged box pendant, and cut a piece of the textured paper to fit inside the pendant perfectly.

4 Use the pencil to lightly mark the background paper in the spot where you want to place each butterfly. Using a toothpick, apply a very small dot of cyanoacrylate glue to the outside of the fold of the first butterfly. Use the tweezers to gently position the butterfly onto the dot on the background and hold it for 10 to15 seconds to let the glue set. Repeat this step with the remaining butterflies.

5 Add several small dots of glue to the inside of the box pendant. Carefully set the completed butterfly assemblage inside the box pendant and hold it for 10 to 15 seconds to let the glue set.

6 Close up the completed pendant and add the chain and clasp set.

Designer *Kathy Sheldon*

Cameo and Dangle Earrings

These earrings, made with purchased cameos (available online and in bead shops), brass settings, and crystal bicones, are eye-catching, while extra light and comfortable to wear.

1 Apply the jewelry adhesive evenly to the flat back of one cameo and press it into one lace-edge cup setting. Repeat with the second cameo and lace-edge cup setting. Set the assemblages aside to dry completely.

2 Thread one gold ball-head headpin through two blue crystal bicones. Make a simple loop with the headpin (see page 28). Repeat to make a second dangle.

materials

- Jewelry adhesive
- 2 resin cameos, 13 x 18 mm
- 2 brass lace-edge cup settings, 13 x 18 mm (the kind with two loops down)
- 2 gold ball-head headpins
- 4 blue crystal bicones
- 2 gold ear wires

tools

- 2 pairs of chain-nose pliers
- Flush wire cutters
- Round-nose pliers

Cameo and Dangle Earrings

3 Carefully open the loop of one dangle, catch the bottom loop of one brass setting, and close the loop. Repeat with the second dangle and second brass setting.

4 Open the loop of one of the ear wires. Catch the top loop of one brass setting in it, then close it. Repeat for the second ear wire and the second brass setting.

Braille Peace
Pendant

Designer Natalka Pavlysh

materials

- Template (page 124)
- White linen 40-count embroidery fabric, approximately 4 x 4 inches (10.2 x 10.2 cm)
- Embroidery hoop
- Embroidery floss in dark khaki*
- 9 size 10° brown seed beads
- Oval three-piece silver frame pendant setting with a bail, 1½ x 1 inch (3.8 x 2.5 cm) (see Note)
- 20-inch (50.8 cm) length of silver chain with clasp

  * Natalka recommends DMC embroidery floss color 3011.

tools

- Disappearing fabric marker
- Embroidery needle or sewing needle that will fit through the seed beads
- Scissors

NOTE: A three-piece frame setting contains a frame, an inside oval, and an oval back piece. If you can only find a two-piece setting, just cut a piece of stiff paper to match the oval back piece and substitute it for the inside oval in steps 5 and 6. If your pendant comes without a bail setting, use a jump ring (if needed) to attach it to the chain.

Braille Peace Pendant

The little seed beads on this pendant are arranged to spell *peace* in Braille.

1 Follow the instructions on page 20 to transfer the template's design onto the embroidery fabric.

2 Center the fabric in the embroidery hoop. Thread the needle with two plies of the floss.

3 Embroider the stem and leaves design using the Backstitch (page 22). Work each stitch over two threads of the embroidery fabric (this means there will be two threads of the embroidery fabric under each stitch). Do not make knots in the embroidery thread because they will show through the fabric and spoil the look. Instead, use an Away Knot (page 21) and leave short ends of floss on the wrong side of the fabric.

4 To add the seed beads, first thread the needle with two plies of the floss. Bring the needle from the wrong side to the right side of the fabric in the lower left-hand corner of the block where the bead is positioned, leaving the short end of the thread on the wrong side. Pick up a bead with your needle, then poke the needle back down through the right side of the fabric in the upper right-hand corner of the same block. Repeat with all nine beads to make the word *peace* in Braille.

5 Use the inside oval from the pendant setting as a guide to cut around the embroidered design, but add about 1 inch (2.5 cm) of fabric around all sides so you end up with a 3½ x 3-inch (8.9 x 7.6 cm) oval of fabric with the embroidered design in the center.

6 Center the embroidered fabric over the inside oval, making sure the edges around the design are even. Fold the fabric onto the wrong side, and cut any excess fabric if necessary.

7 Insert the assemblage into the pendant frame, add the back oval, and secure (the piece shown has little tabs that fold down to secure the assemblage).

8 Add the pendant to a chain with clasps, and the necklace is ready to wear!

Lolita Earrings

Unique findings and glittery balls of polymer clay make these earrings both sweet and elegant.

1 Follow the instructions on page 28 for Making a Wrapped Loop to make one wrapped loop from each 2-inch (5.1cm) piece of wire, but attach one ¾-inch (1.9 cm) length of the flat cable chain to each wire's loop before wrapping.

2 Trim each wire to a ¼-inch (6 mm) length.

3 See page 13 for more on polymer clay. Make a small ball with polymer clay by rolling the clay between your thumb and index finger. Make sure the ball fits inside the bead cap. If it is too small or too big, add or remove a bit of clay and make the ball again until the polymer clay ball fits perfectly inside the bead cap. Leave the ball of clay snug inside the bead cap.

4 Add some cyanoacrylate glue to the end of one wrapped loop assemblage and insert it into the bead cap hole all the way into the polymer clay until the wrapped section of wire reaches the edge of the bead cap.

materials

- 4-inch (10.2 cm) length of 24-gauge craft wire, cut in half
- Two ¾-inch (1.9 cm) lengths of small, flat cable chain
- Small amount of pink or peach polymer clay
- 2 decorative bead caps
- Cyanoacrylate glue
- Clear embossing powder (see Note)
- Decoupage medium
- 2 leaf connectors
- 2 jump rings
- 2 lever-back earring findings

NOTE: To achieve the frosted finish on the polymer beads, Afsaneh uses a blasting abrasive for cleaning aluminum and brass parts that's made from tiny glass beads. Clear embossing powder should give the same effect.

(Tools on next page)

Lolita Earrings

tools

- Wire cutters
- Round-nose pliers
- 2 pairs of flat-nose pliers
- Small bowl
- Small paintbrush (optional)
- Polymer clay bead rack (see Note)

NOTE: Afsaneh recommends using a bead rack (found at craft stores) for baking polymer clay beads. You can also use a foil bread pan pierced with wire.

5 To add the frosted, velvety finish to the polymer clay, add clear embossing powder to a small bowl. Lightly cover the surface of the polymer clay bead with the decoupage medium using a small brush, or just dab a little bit onto the bead and very gently roll it between your thumb and index finger so that the entire surface is coated with glue. Roll the polymer clay bead in the bowl of embossing powder to cover the entire surface.

6 Repeat steps 3 through 5 to make a second bead assemblage.

7 Hang the beads, chains and all, in a polymer clay bead rack. Preheat your oven to 275°F (135°C) or whatever temperature is

recommended for your brand of polymer clay. Bake the beads for 7 minutes on the middle rack of the oven.

8 Take the beads out of the oven and let them cool completely.

9 Attach each connecting chain to a leaf connector with a small jump ring (see photo, right).

10 Connect each leaf connector's loop to one lever-back earring finding's loop (see photo right, again).

Designer *Natalka Pavlysh*

Ukrainian Necklace and Earrings

This jewelry set by a Ukrainian designer is inspired by traditional patterns. Red is lovely, but, then again, blue looks awfully nice, too.

Make the Cross-Stitched Components

1. Following the instructions on page 20, transfer the template's design onto the embroidery fabric five times, leaving at least 1 inch (2.5 cm) around the sides of each one.

2. Center your fabric in the embroidery hoop. Thread the embroidery needle with two plies of the floss.

3. Cross-stitch the designs, being sure to work each stitch over two threads of the embroidery fabric (this means there will be two threads of the embroidery fabric under each stitch). Knots may show through the fabric, so instead begin with an Away Knot (page 21) and end by running your floss back through a few stitches, leaving short ends on the wrong side of the fabric.

4. Cut out the stitched designs leaving about ½ inch (1.3 cm) of fabric around each design so you end up with five ovals of fabric with a cross-stitched design centered in each.

5. Use the oval template to trace and cut out five ovals from the white cardstock or thin cardboard.

materials

- Templates (page 124)
- White linen 40-count embroidery fabric, 6 x 6 inches (15.2 x 15.2 cm)
- Red embroidery floss*
- White cardstock or thin cardboard
- Fabric glue
- 5 bronze lace-edge cup settings, 18 x 25 mm
- 4 bronze jump rings, 5 mm
- 4 size 10° red seed beads
- 13¾-inch (35 cm) length of bronze chain
- 4 bronze jump rings, 3 mm
- 1 bronze jump ring, 8 mm
- 2 bronze ear wires

* Natalka used DMC embroidery floss color 666. Try blue DMC 312 and blue beads for a variation.

(Tools on next page)

Ukrainian Necklace and Earrings

tools

- Disappearing fabric marker
- Ruler
- Embroidery hoop
- Embroidery needle or sewing needle
- Scissors
- Pencil
- 2 pairs of chain-nose or needle-nose pliers
- Wire cutters

6 Center each cardstock oval behind a stitched oval of fabric. Make sure the borders around the cross-stitched design are even, then glue the fabric onto the back of the cardstock or cardboard, cutting any excess fabric if there are folds on the back.

7 Glue each fabric oval inside a lace-edge cup setting. Let dry.

Make the Necklace

1 Using the photo on page 88 for reference, arrange three of the cross-stitched components so you can decide where the two jump rings connecting each piece will go. Open one 5-mm jump ring with two pairs of pliers, hook it over the laced edge at the top of one component, then hook it over the lace edge of the top of the adjacent component, and close the jump ring. Repeat at the bottom of the same components, but this time add one red seed bead to the jump ring before closing it.

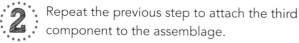
back

2. Repeat the previous step to attach the third component to the assemblage.

3. Cut the bronze chain into two equal halves using the wire cutters.

4. Connect each half of the chain to the upper edge of one of the components with a 3-mm jump ring.

5. Use a 3-mm jump ring to connect the clasp to other end of one length of chain. Connect one 3-mm jump ring and then one 8-mm jump ring to the other end of the length of chain.

Make the Earrings

1. Open the bottom loop of one ear wire.

2. Add one red seed bead, hook the loop through the top scallop of one embroidered setting, and close the loop.

3. Repeat steps 1 and 2 to make the other earring.

Tweet Bracelet

Take a flock of glass bird beads, copper eye pins, and some chain, and you'll have a bracelet to tweet about.

1 Using both pairs of chain-nose pliers, open an eye pin. Slide on the fine copper chain, then close the eye pin. Leaving two large links attached to the eye pin, cut off the rest of the chain.

2 Open another eye pin. Slide on the fine copper chain, then close the eye pin. Leaving *three* large links attached to the eye pin this time, cut off the chain.

3 Repeat steps 1 and 2 until you've attached chain to all 12 eye pins, half of them with two links on them and half with three.

4 Run one of the eye pins through a bird-shaped bead from the top down. Make a wrapped loop (see page 28) below the bead to hold on the eye pin. Repeat so that all of the bird beads are strung onto the eye pins.

5 Using the oval jump rings, attach the wrapped loops with the bird-shaped beads on them to the rolo chain, spacing them evenly across it and leaving at least two unused links at each end. Be sure to attach each of the jump rings on the same side of the link, or the chain will twist and the bracelet won't hang right. If you get any wrong, you can always re-open those jump rings and switch the dangles to the other side.

6 Use a jump ring to attach half of the clasp at each end of the chain.

materials

- 8-inch (20.3 cm) length of fine copper chain
- 6½-inch (16.5 cm) length of copper rolo chain*
- 12 copper eye pins
- 12 bird-shaped glass beads in shades of white, pale blue, and turquoise
- 14 oval copper jump rings
- 1 copper ball-and-socket clasp

  * If you have a large wrist, get 7½ inches (19 cm).

tools

- 2 pairs of chain-nose pliers
- Round-nose pliers
- Wire cutters

NOTE: Rather than building one component at a time, you'll make all of the dangles at once, then attach them to the rolo chain.

Designer Kathy Sheldon

Dahlias and Drops Earrings

Add a bit of bling to dainty dahlia cabochons with glass navettes.
You can purchase them in settings for simple assembly.

materials

- Jewelry adhesive
- 2 ivory dahlia cabochons, 10 mm
- 2 brass round lace-edge settings, 10 mm
- 2 gold jump rings, 5 mm
- 2 red glass navette beads in loop settings
- 2 gold ear wires

tools

- 2 pairs of flat-nose pliers

1 Apply the jewelry adhesive evenly to the flat back of one dahlia cabochon and place it on one round lace-edge setting. Let the adhesive dry completely.

2 Open a jump ring. Hook it through a loop in the dalhia's lace-edge setting and through the loop of one red navette's setting. Close the jump ring.

3 Open the loop on one of the ear wires, and catch it onto the loop in the lace-edge setting that's directly across from the loop the navette is hanging from, then close it. Repeat steps 1 through 3 to make the second earring.

back

Designer Aimee Ray

materials

- Brown and/or blue polymer clay
- Brown and/or blue acrylic paint
- Clear acrylic varnish
- Brown felt, 3 x 3 inches (7.6 x 7.6 cm), or scraps
- Brown thread
- Metal pin back
- White school glue

tools

- Paintbrushes
- Scissors
- Sewing needle

Nest Brooch

Got some scraps of felt laying around? Make like a bird and gather them into a nest. There's something so hopeful about a bird's nest with eggs.

1 Form three small egg shapes approximately ⅜ inch (9.5 mm) long from the polymer clay and gently press them together to make a ¾-inch (1.9 cm) circle. Bake the clay according to the manufacturer's instructions.

2 Paint the eggs in blue or brown, add speckles, and let dry.

3 Coat the eggs with the clear varnish.

4 Cut a 1¼-inch (3.2 cm) circle from the felt. Cut several strips of felt ⅛ inch (3 mm) wide and taper the ends.

5 Sew the felt strips to the felt circle, overlapping them around the edge to form a nest. Don't worry about being too neat—nests are messy! When you've sewn strips all around the edge, add another layer.

6 Stitch a pin back to the back and glue the eggs into the nest.

Designer *Kathy Sheldon*

materials

- Two-part silicone molding putty
- Vintage cameo
- Polymer clay in cream and green
- Jewelry adhesive
- Oval filigree pendant blank (slightly larger than cameo)
- Ring blank with flat surface

tools

- Nonstick work surface
- Oven
- Sandpaper, emery board, or file (optional)
- Cardboard

NOTE: It's easy to find vintage cameos at yard sales and in thrift shops.

Cameo Ring

Love the look of cameos? Create your own from polymer clay — it's easier than you think!

1 Follow the instructions on page 24 to use the two-part silicone molding putty to make a mold from your cameo.

2 Follow the instructions on page 25 to use the cream and green polymer clay to make a cameo. Let the cameo sit for 24 hours before gently sanding or filing the edges (if needed).

3 Apply jewelry adhesive to the back of the cameo, center the cameo over the filigree, and press to adhere. Adjust the cameo if needed so the filigree pendant forms an even "frame" around the cameo.

Cameo Ring

4 Apply jewelry adhesive to the surface of the ring blank, center the filigree oval with the cameo carefully over the ring blank surface, and press to adhere. Let the adhesive dry completely.

tip

- For a super-simple cameo ring, just add a purchased cameo (available at bead shops, online, or recycled from costume jewelry) to a ring blank with jewelry adhesive.

Bohemian Necklace and Earrings

Designer Katherine McGrath

materials

For the Necklace

- Templates (page 125)
- Fabric, approximately 50 x 50 inches (127 x 127 cm) to allow for matching
- Cover buttons with flat backs:

   one 1½ inches (3.8 cm) in diameter

   two 1⅛ inches (2.9 cm) in diameter

   two ¾ inch (1.9 cm) in diameter

   6 to 8 jump rings, 3 mm

- Lace-edge cabochon settings:

   1 cup setting, 38 mm

   2 cup settings, 28 mm

   2 cup settings, 20 mm

- 15-inch (38.1 cm) length of metal chain
- Lobster clasp
- Fabric glue

NOTE: In addition to various sizes of cover buttons, molds, and pushers, most cover-button kits include templates for cutting out fabric to cover the buttons. The templates on page 125 represent the correct sizes needed for the buttons indicated.

Bohemian Necklace

Bold patterned fabric makes this project really stand out. Cover buttons and lace-edge settings make it come together easily.

1 Use the templates to trace the five circles onto the wrong side of the fabric. (Remember to match the fabric pattern, if desired, for the same-size circles.) Cut out the circles.

2 Place the largest circle of fabric right side down on the work surface. Center the 1½-inch (3.8 cm) button cover on the fabric, rounded side down.

3 Push the fabric and button into the 1½-inch (3.8 cm) button mold, fabric side first. Fold the excess fabric over into the hollow part of the button. Place the 1½-inch (3.8 cm) flat backing onto the top of the mold, use the pusher to press the back into the button, and then pop the button out of the mold.

4 Repeat steps 2 and 3 for each of the remaining four buttons, using their corresponding cut-fabric circles, button covers, backs, molds, and pushers.

5 Open a jump ring with two pairs of needle-nose pliers and hook it through one loop on the largest 38-mm cabochon setting and one loop on one of the 28-mm settings. Close the jump ring.

tools

For the Necklace

- Fabric pen or disappearing fabric marker
- Scissors
- Cover-button kits with molds and pushers sized to fit your buttons (available at fabric stores)
- 2 pairs of needle-nose pliers
- Ruler

6 Locate the loop directly across from the jump ring on the 28-mm setting above, and hook another jump ring through that loop and to one of the loops on one of the 20-mm settings.

7 Repeat steps 5 and 6 with the remaining settings, working on the opposite side of the 38-mm setting.

8 Use the needle-nose pliers to separate the chain into two 7½-inch (19 cm) pieces. Use a jump ring to attach one end of one chain to one of the loops on the 20-mm setting. Repeat for the other chain on the other side of the necklace, attaching it to the corresponding loop on the other 20-mm setting so that the necklace hangs evenly.

9 Attach the lobster clasp to the final link on one side of the chain, or if the links are too small, attach the lobster clasp to one side with a jump ring and add another jump ring to the other side of the chain.

10 Attach a jump ring to each of the two bracelet ends using the remaining thread loops. Attach the jump ring to each end of the clasp.

tip

- If any buttons are too tight to fit in the setting, use the pliers to bend the loops containing jump rings out just slightly.

materials

For the Earrings

- Templates (page 125)
- Fabric, approximately 25 x 25 inches (63.5 x 63.5 cm) to allow for matching
- Cover buttons with flat backs:

  two ½ inch (1.3 cm) in diameter

  two ¾ inch (1.9 cm) in diameter
- 2 jump rings, 3 mm
- Lace-edge cabochon settings:

  2 cup settings, 20 mm

  2 flat settings, 13 mm
- 2 earring hooks
- Fabric glue

tools

- Fabric pen or disappearing fabric marker
- Scissors
- Cover-button kits with molds and pushers sized to fit your buttons (available at fabric stores)
- 2 pairs of needle-nose pliers

Bohemian Earrings

1 Follow steps 1 through 3 for the necklace to make the four covered buttons for the earrings.

2 Use the pliers to gently bend one of the loops on the 20-mm setting down so that it lies perpendicular to the other loops (see the photos for reference). Bend every fourth loop in the same way. Repeat this with the other 20-mm setting for the second earring.

3 Hook a jump ring through one of the bent loops on the 20-mm setting. Hook the same jump ring through one of the loops on the 13-mm flat setting. Use the pliers to close the loop. Repeat this with the remaining two settings.

4 Use the pliers to slightly open the loop on the earring hook. Locate the loop directly across from the jump ring on the 13-mm setting. Hook this loop onto the open earring hook. Use pliers to close the earring hook. Repeat for the other earring.

5 Apply the fabric glue around the base of each setting. Position the buttons in the settings, making sure the fabric patterns match, if desired, and let dry completely.

materials

- Template (page 124)

- 18 x 25 mm oval antique bronze pendant bezel

- Decoupage medium or clear packing tape (see step 3)

- Double-sided tape

- Disposable gloves

- Two-part resin

- 2 small graduated plastic cups (these usually come with the resin but are also available in pharmacies)

- 2 wood craft sticks

- 4 antiqued brass jump rings, 3.5 mm or larger

- 20-inch (50.8 cm) length (or preferred length) of vintage brass or antiqued chain

- 1 antiqued brass lobster clasp, 10 mm or larger (depending on chain's size)

- 1 vintage or antiqued brass two-loop connector finding

- 1 pendant of your choice with a loop at the top

(Tools on page 108)

All the new products on the market make working with resin easier than ever. The results, as you can see with this Foxy Pendant, are worth the little extra effort resin involves.

Make the Resin Pendant

1 Either photocopy or scan and print the template in color. For best results, let the printout dry overnight.

2 Cut the image out carefully, place it in the bezel to test it for size, and trim it if necessary.

3 It's best to seal the image so it doesn't react with the resin. Either coat the image—front, back, and edges—with several coats of decoupage medium (let the medium dry between each coat), or seal it between two pieces of clear packaging tape (make sure the tape extends a tiny bit past the edges so the resin can't seep through).

4 Use the double-sided tape to place the sealed image in the bottom of the pendant bezel (make sure the pendant's loop is at the top!). Place the bezel on a level surface.

5 Wearing the disposable gloves, follow the manufacturer's instructions to mix your specific resin. Have the timer nearby to set when stirring—it's important to stir for the exact amount of time recommended by the manufacturer. Here are the basic steps for most resins:

- Mark one cup with pour lines (depending on the ratio needed), place it on a level surface, and pour part A and then part B of the resin into the cup.

- Use a wooden craft stick to stir the mixture (usually for two minutes), continually scraping from the sides and bottom of the cup. Don't whip as you stir or you'll add bubbles to the resin—see Bubble Trouble, page 109.

Foxy Resin Pendant

tools

- Photocopier or scanner and printer
- Scissors
- Small paintbrush
- Timer
- Marker
- 2 pairs of chain-nose pliers

tip

- In a hurry? Just buy premade resin pendants online at shops such as Happy Jewelry Supplies (who were kind enough to share their instructions with us), and add jump rings, a clasp, a connector, and chain to make a necklace. See etsy.com/shop/happysupplies.

- Pour the mixture into a new cup and use a new wooden craft stick to stir for an additional amount of time (usually one minute).

- Let the mixture rest for a minute so most of the bubbles dissolve.

6 Pour the resin into the bezel slowly, taking care not to overfill. Let the resin settle for a minute and then add a few more drops to fill if needed.

7 Let the resin cure undisturbed for the amount of time recommended by the manufacturer—don't cheat! It can take up to 48 hours for some resins to completely harden.

Make the Necklace

1 Use the pliers and one jump ring to attach the lobster clasp to the last open link of the 20-inch (50.8 cm) chain.

2 Attach another jump ring to the other end of the chain.

3 Attach a third jump ring to one loop of the connector finding and the center loop of the necklace chain. (If you are using a very fine chain, slip the jump ring around the entire chain instead).

4 Open the last jump ring and slip it through the bottom hole of the connector finding and then through the pendant's loop. Close the jump ring.

Bubble Trouble

Bubbles are the bane of resin-jewelry makers. Here are some tips for preventing and dissolving bubbles:

- Pretend you're being graded in Chem Lab 101, and follow the manufacturer's instructions precisely for all steps.

- Don't whip when mixing—stir and scrape instead.

- Let the resin mixture sit for a minute before pouring

- Remove bubbles from a project that's curing by popping them with a straight pin (carefully, or you may disturb the surface and add bubbles instead!), blowing very carefully on the resin through a plastic straw (the carbon monoxide in your breath should do the trick), or placing the curing resin under a warm lamp.

Designer *Sandie Zimmerman*

Lazy Daisy Cuff

materials

- Template (page 125)
- Pewter gray wool felt, about 20 x 5 inches (50.8 x 12.7 cm)
- Embroidery floss in orange, red-violet, red, and dark gray*
- Metal snap

  * Sandie used DMC embroidery floss in colors 976, 915, 498, and 413.

tools

- Scissors
- Tissue paper
- Straight pins
- Large embroidery needle

Just a few simple stitches make up the cheerful design on this felt cuff.

1 Cut two 9½ x 2½-inch (24.1 x 6.4 cm) pieces of pewter gray felt.

2 Trace the template onto the tissue paper and pin the paper to the front of one piece of felt.

3 Embroider the design (except for the straight-stitched border) with the floss colors and stitches indicated (see page 113).

4 Align the second piece of felt behind the piece you just embroidered. Sew the two pieces of felt together using the Straight Stitch (page 22) and dark gray floss, but leave the ends unsewn.

5 Follow the outside border to cut both pieces of felt and form the shape of the bracelet.

6 Remove the tissue paper.

Lazy Daisy Cuff

7 Fit the bracelet onto your wrist and mark where both of the snaps should be sewn.

8 Sew one side of the snap on the unsewn wrong side of the bracelet and one on the embroidered right side of the bracelet.

9 Finish sewing the outlines on both ends to close the bracelet.

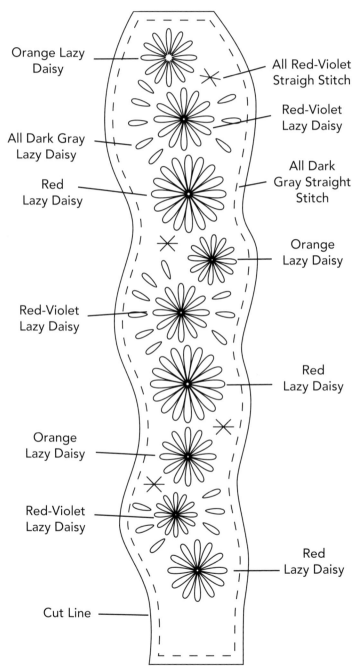

Orange Lazy Daisy

All Red-Violet Straigh Stitch

Red-Violet Lazy Daisy

All Dark Gray Lazy Daisy

All Dark Gray Straight Stitch

Red Lazy Daisy

Orange Lazy Daisy

Red-Violet Lazy Daisy

Red Lazy Daisy

Orange Lazy Daisy

Red-Violet Lazy Daisy

Red Lazy Daisy

Cut Line

Peach Coral and Pearl Earrings

These earrings with freshwater pearls and peach coral rondelles are the perfect project for practising hammering skills.

1 With the wire cutters, cut the 6-inch (15.2 cm) wire in half, resulting in two 3-inch (7.6 cm) lengths.

2 Add one pearl to one head pin. With round-nose pliers, make a basic wire-wrapped loop (see page 28) on the head pin above the pearl.

3 Place the mandrel over the center of the 3-inch (7.6 cm) length of wire. Secure the mandrel so that it doesn't move. Hold both ends of the wire with your fingers; evenly lift both ends of the wire up around the mandrel. Slightly cross the ends of the wire to create and hold a teardrop shape. Remove the mandrel from the wire frame.

4 Place the teardrop frame flat onto the bench block with the top pointing away from you. Hold it on the right-hand side with your fingers.

5 Using the riveting hammer and starting at the top of the left side of the frame, gently hammer about ⅝ inch (1.6 cm) of the left-hand side of the frame to slightly flatten the wire.

6 Remove the teardrop frame from the bench block and hold the frame so that the front of the hammered side is facing away from you.

materials

- 6-inch (15.2 cm) length of 14-karat, 22-gauge, half-hard round gold-filled wire

- 2 round peach freshwater pearls, 7.5 mm

- Two 14-karat gold-filled 24-gauge head pins, 2 inches (5.1 cm) long, with a 1.5-mm ball

- 20 faceted peach coral rondelle beads, 4 mm

- Two 14-karat gold-filled French ear wires with 1.5-mm ball

tools

- Wire cutters

- Ruler

- Round-nose pliers

- Mandrel, size 17.5 mm (size 7 on a ring mandrel)

- Steel bench block or anvil

- Small riveting hammer with a face diameter of 8 to 9 mm

- Chain-nose pliers

Peach Coral and Pearl Earrings

7 On the hammered side, place the top of the wire ¼ inch (6 mm) from the tip of the round-nose pliers and form a simple loop (see page 28), curving it outward away from you. The tip of the loop should touch the hammered frame.

8 Now hold the frame so that the hammered side is on your left with the front facing you. Add the beads to the wire on the right side in the following order: five coral beads, one pearl dangle, five coral beads.

9 Place the right-hand side of the frame on the bench block and use the riveting hammer to gently hammer the portion of wire that extends above the beads. Starting from the top, slightly flatten the wire.

10 On the right-hand side, place the top of the wire ¼ inch (6 mm) from the tip of the round-nose pliers and form a simple loop, curving it outward to the right. The tip of the loop should touch the outside of the hammered frame.

11 Face the front of the frame toward you and use the chain-nose pliers to open the left side loop (formed in step 7) by pulling it slightly upward.

12 Gently pull the top left side of the frame over to the top right side and link the left side loop to the right-hand side frame, directly under the right-hand side loop. With the chain-nose pliers, gently close the left-hand side loop so that it touches the hammered frame.

13 At this point, the frame will be a little lopsided. Gently pull the frame back into shape using the pliers and your fingers as needed. The finished shape won't be a perfect teardrop, but it should look balanced.

14 Open the loop of the French ear wire by opening it slightly outward. Attach it to the top loop of the beaded drop hoop, then close the loop of the ear wire.

15 Repeat steps 2 through 14 to make the second earring.

Designers *Alicia Henson* and *Jessica Berner*

Dandelion Wish Necklace

Make a wish on a dandelion seed and let it float off to come true.

1 Using the tweezers, carefully place the dandelion seeds in the glass vial. Arrange the seeds to your liking.

2 Apply a small amount of clear jewelry adhesive to the center of the top of the cork.

3 Screw the eye screw directly into the drop of glue on the top of the cork. Allow the glue to dry for one to two hours before proceeding.

4 Carefully push the cork into the glass vial. If you've glued the cork to the vial, let it dry for an hour or two.

5 Open one of the jump rings with two pairs of chain-nose pliers and attach the "wish" charm and the ball chain. Close the jump ring.

6 Open the other jump ring and attach the eye screw (on the glass vial) and the ball chain. Close the jump ring.

materials

- Dandelion seeds
- 1 mini glass vial with cork (you can find these online and at craft stores)
- Clear jewelry adhesive
- 1 tiny silver eye screw
- 2 silver jump rings, 6 mm
- Silver "wish" charm
- 18-inch (45.7 cm) length of silver ball chain with a connector

tools

- Tweezers
- 2 pairs of flat-nose pliers

tip

- You can leave your cork unglued if you want to be able to take out your dandelion seeds to make wishes. Otherwise, add a bit of glue along the middle of the cork's side edge before proceeding to step 4.

Painted Picture Choker

Air-dry clay is the perfect canvas for a wearable piece of art.

materials

- Small amount of air-dry clay (such as Paperclay)
- 1 round silver-frame two-loop bezel or connector charm, ¾ inch (1.9 cm) in diameter
- Watercolor or acrylic paints
- Jewelry adhesive
- 1 glass bead to coordinate with the artwork, 6 mm
- 1 silver head pin, 1 inch (2.5 cm)
- 1 silver jump ring, 6 mm
- 1 choker-style necklace

tools

- Tiny paintbrushes
- Two pairs of chain-nose pliers
- Round-nose pliers

1. Form a pea-size amount of clay into a ball and press it flat into the silver frame of the connector charm until it touches the edges. Allow it to dry thoroughly.

2. Paint a tiny picture, scene, or just a pretty abstract color design on the clay disk. Let the paint dry completely.

3. Glue the painted clay into the frame so that its loops are at the top and bottom. Let the glue dry thoroughly.

4. Slide the head pin through the bead and then through the bottom ring of the silver frame. Make a simple loop (see page 28) to attach the bead to the frame. Close the loop.

5. Attach the jump ring to the silver frame's top loop. Close the jump ring.

6. String the charm onto a choker-style necklace.

Templates
copy at 100%

Embroidered Felt Pin

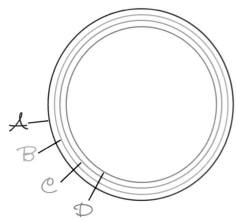

A
B
C
D

Fabric Scrap Necklaces

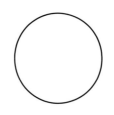

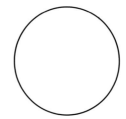

Retro Button Bracelet

Hedgehog Shrink Plastic Necklace

Button Blossom Earrings

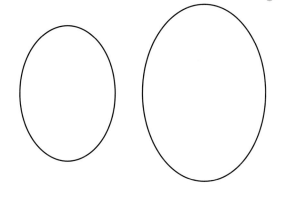

Butterfly Specimen Locket

Templates

copy at 100%

Braille Peace Necklace

Foxy Pendant

Ukrainian Necklace and Earrings

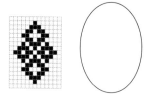

Templates

copy at 100%

Bohemian Necklace and Earrings

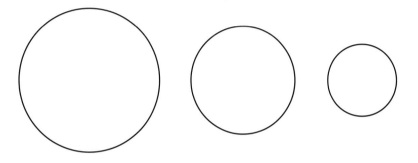

Lazy Daisy Cuff

About the Designers

Paola Benenati is a native of Uruguay but currently lives in Barcelona, Spain. She is a graphic designer, jewelry designer, and crafter. She has created her own jewelry all her life, but she discovered real satisfaction when she started to sell what she makes. She loves creating for others and experimenting with all kinds of materials and colors.

Jessica Berner and Alicia Henson began creating together to honor their sister Sarah, who died in 2008. The memory of dandelion puffs, which the girls called "wishers," led them to one of their first creations, the glass-vial dandelion pendant. Many of the items in their shop are inspired by Sarah, and the dandelion is incorporated into many of their designs. Alicia and Jessica believe in focusing on the positive, living life to the fullest, and being creative. Visit their Etsy shop at www.wisher21.etsy.com or stop in to say hello at www.facebook.com/Wisher21.

Jennifer M. Burgess originally from Dayton, Ohio, is a military wife who has lived in five states and currently calls Tampa, Florida, home. She loves to spend her free time creating jewelry that is casual, versatile, and feminine. Jennifer began beading and jewelry making soon after her mom and stepdad first took her to a bead store. You may contact her at bludaisyjewelry@gmail.com and view her work at www.bludaisyjewelry.etsy.com.

Melissa Davison lives in Dayton, Ohio, under a mountain of embroidery floss, yarn, felt, and fabric. Her husband and small daughter lovingly support her obsession with all things handmade. Her embroidered jewelry, accessories, and wall art are sold in her Etsy shop, www.sewsweetstitches.etsy.com.

Kaitryne Durham's career began in the 1990s with a high-end silver collection she designed and sold in boutique shops in New York and Los Angeles. Her love for everything vintage and her vast collection of vintage pendants and beads led to the birth of Chloe's Vintage Jewelry. She lives in Minneapolis. Visit her shop at www.chloesvintagejewelry.etsy.com. She also sells vintage brass pendants and findings at www.myshangrila.etsy.com.

Sonya Fabricant loves the trickiness of working with feathers—each one unpredictable and exquisitely different. She began Headfeathers as a high school kid growing up in Eugene, Oregon. Now she plans to continue with the feather business as she finishes her undergraduate degree in the Northwest. You can find her earrings at www.etsy.com/shop/sonyapaige.

Katherine McGrath is a crafter by hobby and a teacher at heart. She enjoys nature, gardening, and cooking. She has an online shop, Clammy's Closet (www.etsy.com/shop/clammyscloset), featuring fabric button jewelry and accessories. She lived in Florida for most of her life and recently moved to Winston-Salem, North Carolina.

Nathalie Mornu studied at the Appalachian Center for Crafts in Smithville, Tennessee, then earned a mass communications degree before joining Lark Crafts. She's created projects for Lark publications as varied as stitched pot holders, beaded jewelry, a reupholstered mid-century chair, a scarecrow made from old cutlery,

and a gingerbread igloo. Nathalie lives in Asheville, North Carolina. Her author credits include *Leather Jewelry*, *Contemporary Bead & Wire Jewelry*, and *Chains Chains Chains*.

Natalka Pavlysh lives in Kryvyi Rih, Ukraine, and runs an Etsy shop at www.skrynka.etsy.com. As a child she learned to knit, crochet, and sew, but embroidery became her true passion, particularly cross-stitch. She's inspired by traditional Ukrainian designs, drawing from the rich tradition of homemade Ukrainian fabrics and handmade embroidery.

Linda Stone Ray is a full-time jewelry designer, and most days she can be found in her waterfront studio on the North Carolina coast. Using gemstones, pearls, crystals, and lampwork glass beads in almost every shape and size imaginable, she designs jewelry in styles ranging from big and bold to dainty and delicate. Visit her studio website at www.stoneraystudio.com.

Morgan Shooter started Miss Bluebird Creations in 2007 as a bird-obsessed crafter with a penchant for anything retro. She resides in sunny Gainesville, Florida, with her two cats, and she often attends local craft shows. Check out her Etsy shop at www.missbluebirdcreations.com

Afsaneh Tajvidi is a full-time artist with a range of interests: jewelry, painting, clay sculpture, photography, and more. She was born and raised in Tehran, Iran, in a family of artists and emmigrated to Canada in 2006. She lives with her husband in Toronto and shares her art and creative ideas in her blog, www.joojoo.me. She also sells her art prints and jewelry in her online Etsy shops, www.joojoo.etsy.com and www.joojooland.etsy.com.

Donni Webber grew up in South Africa, surrounded by animals and wilderness. She's lived in Ireland, England, New Zealand, and now, California, where she has settled with her Kiwi husband and two children. See more of her lovely crafts at www.fairyfolk.etsy.com and www.theMagicOnions.com.

Sandie Zimmerman always felt out of place in the world until she put a needle and thread in her hand. These days, she spends much of her time sitting on her porch in Noblesville, Indiana, stitching the day away. You can find more about her at www.lovemaude.wordpress.com and her work at www.lovemaude.etsy.com.

About the Authors

Aimee Ray loves all types of art and crafts and is always trying something new. Besides embroidery, she dabbles in illustration, crochet, needle felting, sewing, and doll customizing. Aimee's home is in Northwest Arkansas where she has a view of the Ozark mountains from her backyard. She lives with her husband, Josh, their baby son, and two big dogs.

Aimee has written three books on contemporary embroidery designs: *Doodle Stitching: Embroidery and Beyond*, *Doodle Stitching*, and *Doodle-Stitching: The Motif Collection*, and she has contributed to many other Lark titles. See more of her work at www.dreamfollow.com and follow her daily crafting endeavors at www.littledeartracks.blogspot.com.

Kathy Sheldon writes, edits, and packages craft books. She grew up on a farm in New England, so making things by hand comes naturally to her. She's happiest when creating, whether it's a shrink plastic bracelet, a poem, a row of sweet peas, or a book about gardening or crafts. She's written and edited many books, including *Shrink! Shrank! Shrunk: Making Shrink Plastic Jewelry*, *Fa la la la Felt!*, and *Heart-Felt Holidays*. Connecticut, New York City, Seattle, and Charleston, South Carolina, have all been home, but the mountains of Asheville, North Carolina, keep calling her back. When she's not there, you can usually find her at her cottage in Maine, where she's the first to jump in the lake in the spring and the last one to leave the water in the fall.

Acknowledgments

The authors would like to thank:

- The talented and generous designers who shared their work with us. We can't thank them enough, and we can't encourage you enough visit their shops and blogs (see page 126) to see more of their terrific work.

- Long-admired map-maker and editor Jane Crosen for giving us permission to use one of her many beautiful maps to make the Map Rings on page 51. See more of Jane's exquisite work at www.mainemapmaker.com.

- Sparrow Graphics for allowing us to use their image for the Foxy Resin Pendant on page 106. Check out their other wonderful images at www.sparrowgraphic.etsy.com. The owners also sell jewelry findings at ladyjazz.etsy.com.

- The owners of Happy Jewelry Supplies for sharing their technique for making resin pendants with us. You can find their ready-made pendants and other jewelry supplies at www.happyjewelrysupplies.com and www.etsy.com/shop/happysupplies.

- Hannah Doyle, Kathy Brock, and Karen Levy for editorial help on the book.

- A big shout out to photographer and kick-boxer extraordinaire Cynthia Shaffer for working so hard and snapping such lovely pictures.

- Many thanks to Carol Barnao for her lovely book design and for being so sweet while putting up with many not-so-simple requests.

Credits

Art Director
Carol Barnao

Photographer
Cynthia Shaffer

Cover Designer
Laura Palese

Editorial Assistant
Hannah Doyle

Art Intern
Tanya Johnson

Index